AF445782

PRAISE FOR MY COUNTRY, MY TAKE

I loved "My Country, My Take" because I related to every page of it... growing up stories, famous events, celebrities, my favorite Presidents, what is right and wrong with America... it is a CLASSIC! *Steven Dahl*

Richard Lira is a true American Son. He is a product of what is great about our family, our country and true American heroes, like our military and law enforcement. I am proud to stand next to him as he tells it like it is about our wonderful nation! *Frank Postelwhite*

As I read Richard's book, I cried tears of joy, excitement, pride and love for America. He is an author that makes you feel everything you are reading because you are not just reading words on a page, you are *living* it! *Joyce Bentley*

MY COUNTRY, MY TAKE

Richard Lira
My Country, My Take

Published by BooxAi

ISBN: 978-965-577-949-3

MY COUNTRY, MY TAKE

THE JOURNEY OF AN AMERICAN SON

RICHARD LIRA

I dedicate this book to my most precious assets, my children.

Without you, my life would have no meaning or direction. You helped me along the way with advice, motivation, and guidance to make me a better person, and help rescue me from the dark path that I was on.

You may not even know this, but it was you that made me strong and worthwhile. You were the ones that gave me the strength to become a better man.

Thank you.

CONTENTS

INTRODUCTION

This is the journey of a young boy's life growing up in the inner-city neighborhoods of Los Angeles and how the ghetto can make your life a living hell.

Like many other kids, I dreamed of becoming a famous athlete.

In the early 60s, I can remember as a kid watching the Dodgers, Lakers, Rams, and USC football. I wanted to be just like the legends, Wilt Chamberlain, Jerry West, Sandy Koufax, Don Drysdale, Roman Gabriel, and Mike Garrett.

We come into this life full of hopes of what we would like our life to become. As children, we play make-believe, trying on different roles to see if and how they fit.

They say hindsight is 20-20. But I have found that time takes off the sharp edges of those things we think would be best forgotten. It rounds off the corners and gives a mature perspective that can only be gained through living and learning.

This book is a gift to my children and to others, including you, who may find it insightful in life.

It is my hope that it will help them avoid some of the sharp edges that may snag you and hold you back from *your* dreams.

SPECIAL THANKS

Here are some wonderful individuals who believed in me and made my life (and this book!) possible.

First and foremost, I would like to give thanks to my Lord who has always watched over me and my family through good and bad times in my lifetime.

I would like to thank my wonderful parents for bringing me into this world and always being there for me in time of need.

I would like to thank my wonderful children for making me so proud of them and making me feel worth throughout my life, you have made me so very proud of you.

A special thanks to all the men and women that I have served with in the military and in Law Enforcement who have always had my back and made me a better leader.

To my brother Ray who served with the 101st Airborne division and convinced me to go Airborne, and his wife JoJo, who I looked to as my fourth sister, thank you.

To my sisters, Louise, Martha, and Rosemary who were there for me when in need, Thank you.

To Rhonda who always made me feel like family, thank you so very much.

A special thanks to Christine Lorkowski who helped me through a very difficult time while recovering from a major surgery, thank you Chris.

To Tim Marks, CEO of the executive protection company, who gave me my first shot in the business. Thank you brother.

To Jerry Finchum, Operations Lieutenant (Retired) for having me in his prayers and being a great mentor, thank you Sir.

To Steve Kirby, Patrol supervisor (Retired) for always being available when I was in need of help, never a dull moment working with you brother, thanks Kirby.

To Micheal Kandoll, Chief of police (Retied) for being so understanding with your department and working along side with your officers, thank you Sir.

To Ralph Bizzle, Department Training Coordinator (Retired) for the great friendship that we share and most of all for your help along the way, thank you brother.

To Patrick Hurley, Award winning Television producer and ghostwriter, without your help this book would not be possible, thank you my friend.

CHAPTER ONE

MY AMAZING PARENTS

"When you look into your mother's eyes, you know that is the purest love you can find on this earth."

I am the son of Mr. Joseph Simon and Evangeline Lira, two of the greatest parents one could have.

Physically, they were like Mutt and Jeff, dad was over six tall and mom stood under five feet tall.

Unfortunately, I didn't see or spend much time with my father. The times that I did spend with him were memorable.

I was always happy to say he was my dad. My father was a blue-collar worker who served our country in the military.

There is something very special about a soldier.

My mother mostly worked as a housewife raising her children and sometimes working side jobs.

Back then, mothers were to take care of the family at home and the men worked to support them.

Due to the Feminist Movement of the 60s, times have dramatically changed. But in my day, my father was often away from home, and my mother provided us with the daily necessities we needed.

I honestly don't know how my parents were able to get by financially.

It was a difficult economic time in our East LA neighborhood. But they always found a way to get what they needed for their children, whether it was birthdays, holidays, special occasions, or school supplies, we always had them.

It wasn't until I began to get older that I realized that my father was not around as much, but my mother was *always* there when I needed something.

When I was ill, she was the one that cared for me and made things feel so much better,

I don't know what it is, but mothers have this quality about them to make everything better.

They are doctors when you're sick and they are the bank when you need money.

My mother was everything to me and she asked for nothing but the gift of her children.

My dad did teach me some things as I was growing up, but very little, since he was never around that much.

But some of the things he would say to me as a child, I still embrace today.

My mother was my superstar, for an uneducated woman, she was an overflowing font of knowledge,

Mom was a celebrity and didn't even know it.

She was an entertainer, singer, dancer and performed with some of the biggest Latin stars of all time. I didn't find this out until after she had passed away.

My sister invited me to her home and told me, "Mom wanted you to have these items."

They were scrapbooks of my mother's performances and shows she had performed in while I was growing up.

There were dozens and dozens of articles, pictures, and newspaper clippings celebrating her shows with audiences. I was overwhelmed in seeing them.

Not only was my mother a great entertainer, but in demand from the industry, she was a stunningly beautiful lady.

I can honestly say that my musical background came from my mother, "la Mesquita," translated in English, "the little doll," and she was!

I drew my inspiration from her. She would always tell me, "Son, you can become anything you want to be. You will just have to work hard for it!"

My mother was right.

Even when my mother was not feeling good, she was always there for me and made sure I had what I needed at the time.

Both my parents lived through the Great Depression and had managed to survive the hard economic times, just getting by from day to day, and making huge sacrifices for the children they loved.

 We as children don't really appreciate what our parents did for us until we become parents ourselves.

Now that I am a dad, I understand what my parents went through to make sure we had what we needed.

I owe them a lifetime of gratitude, which I could never repay.

To my mother and father, I love and miss you both, until we meet again in heaven.

I come from a very strong Catholic background, and I passionately believe in our Lord!

He has taken care of me and my children for years. I was never perfect in serving Him, but I never stopped loving Him.

I was the youngest sibling and by the time I became aware of my existence, my brothers and sisters were grown, so in essence, I was an "only."

I was too young to really understand what was going on around me. All I knew was when I needed shoes, clothes, or something to eat, my mother made sure I had it.

How she did it, I had no idea, but she somehow made it happen.

She was an uneducated lady who could not read or write, but she made up for it with her grit and perseverance.

She was an amazing human being.

The East L.A. area and surroundings we lived in were saturated with gangs, drugs, shootings, and a whole lot more.

It wasn't Mayberry, it was a war zone.

Things got so bad I can remember going into the kitchen at times to find something to eat, opening the refrigerator for some milk, and it was *sour.*

There were numerous times I didn't enjoy a good meal for days.

We subsisted on Cream of Wheat, eggs, and water. That was my daily intake of nutrition, for the most part.

Several days a month, I didn't eat at all.

As bad as it got, my mom instilled an attitude from an early age to always care for others.

During that time, I was attending Sheridan Elementary School in East LA. I remember on those hot summer days on the playground we would play kickball, tetherball, and other fun things.

Growing up with sports was such a joy to me.

At times I can remember some of the other kids would make fun of me because some of my clothes were not up to fashion as the others.

We were poor. I washed my clothes every other day I arrived home from school since they were the same ones I would wear the next day.

At times I would be afraid to take my shoes off in class when asked because my shoes and socks had holes in them.

I was embarrassed my classmates would make fun of me.

I was ashamed, but I never faulted my mother who was uneducated and worked so hard to keep me fed and pay the bills with what she had.

I don't remember my father being with us in our home during that time in my life. I do recall my brothers and sisters coming and going, but most of the time it was just my mother and me.

Mom and I watched our favorite shows on TV, like Gunsmoke (as Festus reminded us, "When you learn a thing a day you store up smart"), The Andy Griffith Show. We loved ("one bullet Barney!"), The Beverly Hillbillies (Granny's insight, "It ain't Ellie Mae's *shoulders* popping the buttons on her blouse!"), (Hogan's Heroes ("I know NOTHING!"), Mister Rogers ("As human beings, our job in life is to help people"), Engineer Bill and his Cartoon Express, and of course, Batman ("Holy Astringent Plum-Like Fruit, Batman!")

Robin outdid himself on that phrase!

Mom and I would sit there talking and eating what food we had and enjoying each other's company.

A mother and son daily reunion.

But personally, I struggled.

Even at a young age, I was already starting to do things wrong,

In elementary school, I began cutting classes. Evidently, the academic lessons were not holding my attention and I wanted more *action!*

I started to become a problem child in school, and at home, I would walk alone, not caring about anything or anyone.

I would walk the streets all day after school, up and down Brooklyn Avenue. in the East LA area, in and out of stores with no purpose and no guidance.

That was life for most kids in the ghetto areas of LA.

We were constantly reminded that there was no one there to keep us on the straight and narrow, no matter how much they tried.

We had to learn to figure things out on our own.

Gangs were everywhere in the 'hood, and I had several friends that were members, but I never joined a gang.

My mom would have taken me to task for that! (or have my uncle or brother handle it, which they did at times).

She did everything she could to keep me out of trouble, but I was as stubborn and hard-headed as a bucking Bronco in a rodeo pit.

I became very street smart at a very early age.

Had it not been for my upbringing in such a hostile ghetto area, I don't think I would have made it very far success-wise.

Those ups and downs growing up helped me to become a *survivor* in life.

I look back on it now and realize that someone was looking out for me, and I don't mean my mother.

Oh, she was always looking out for me, but there was something else, a higher power was in my corner, and we all knew Who that was!

While living at 2517 Folsom Street in Los Angeles, I can look back on it, living in the ghetto. I was on the street named *Folsom*, Johnny Cash much?

How funny is that?

While I was growing up and still living with my mother, I would spend time with her, taking the bus into the city and going to places like Little Tokyo, Chinatown, Olvera Street, and historic El Pueblo De Los Angeles.

There was the iconic Union Station, Clifton's Cafeteria, Philippe's original beef dip, and the entertaining amusement of the Observatory in Griffith Park.

We not only had Disneyland, but we also had two other amusement parks, Pacific Ocean Park (P.O.P). and The Pike.

There were the La Brea Tar Pits, MacArthur Park, Bunker Hill with its Angel's flight, the world's shortest railway, and the Watts Towers, with its 17 interconnected sculptural edifices, to name a few.

LA was loaded with iconic attractions, especially for kids.

Those were all landmarks in and around the city that I remembered as a child.

My mother would make it a point to take me to those venues even though she could not afford it.

She knew that I enjoyed going to those places, so she did what she could to make it happen.

She was a great mom. She was a 4'11, pepper pot, with brown eyes and a fiery passion to enjoy life!

My mother loved performing on stage and lit up audiences wherever she went.

She was charismatic, fearless, and thrived on challenges. Audiences adored her.

I adored her. I could not have been prouder of her as a son.

CHAPTER TWO

ONCE, TWICE, THREE TIMES A FAMILY!

"**There is nothing more beautiful than someone who goes out of their way to make life beautiful for others.**"

As I was growing up, I met the most incredible group of people, Mr. & Mrs. Robert and Carmen Munoz and their awesome kids, who would end up being the family I never had at home while I was growing up as a child.

They lived next door to us, and they had children of their own, Bobby, Sandy, Art, Charlie, Lola, Desiree, and Martin.

If it had not been for them, who knows where I would have ended up.

I am so thankful to them for being a part of my life. They included me in their family functions and gave me my first true feeling of a family while growing up in the hood.

This was the family connection that I had been missing with my *own* brothers and sisters.

The Munoz kids were closer to my *age* than my siblings, and we had a lot more in common.

Through the Munoz family, I met another incredible family that took me in as one of their own, Mr. & Mrs. Richard and Tina Jimenez.

They had six children of their own, who would become my other family I never had as a child growing up. My brothers and sisters Jimenez, Cecilia, Richard, Olivia, Phillip, Elizabeth, and Sylvia,

I owe so much to these two families, even a lifetime of gratitude and thanks.

Mr. Munoz and Mr. Jimenez both played a major role in my life as the father figures I never really had as a child.

They were there for me, and their children were my brothers and sisters that I never had at home.

Mrs. Carmen Munoz and Mrs. Tina Jimenez were the mothers I could turn to when my mother was not around.

Instead of being a latch-key kid, I had a total of *seventeen* brothers and sisters to hang out with and five parents to look after me!

But make no mistake, I only had one real mother whom I adored, and she never let me down.

She was my loving and beautiful mother Evangeline (Angie) who was known as La Munequita (The Doll) to family and friends.

But she was a popular entertainer and always performing, and a vulnerable boy like me needed surrogate parents and families to support me.

Had they not been there, living in a rough neighborhood, I could have been in a world of trouble.

You need to understand that growing up in the hood was not like a middle-class white suburb in America.

A young person was constantly on edge in East L.A., constantly dealing with financial poverty, gangs, and violence.

Feeling safe in the 'hood was rarely an option.

So to have two strong support systems of families was vitally important here. I was surrounded by adults and children that served as a buffer with all the perils of life pressing down around me.

My first day of school was at Hollenbeck Junior High, a school located in the heart of East Los Angeles.

I can remember it was a very hot summer day with all the students running around like chickens without a head.

The place looked like a prison because the perimeter fences of the school were very high with barbed wire at the top in some areas of the school.

I'm not sure if this was to keep students in or a design to keep the local gang members out.

For the next three years of my life, I will be going to this school.

To make matters more intriguing, my hormones started to kick in. I was starting to have an interest in the ladies now, and there were plenty of them around!

I was a very shy person and unsure of how to communicate with them. This was one of my downfalls in the romance department.

The one thing I *did* notice was that the girls were into guys who were involved in sports. For whatever reason, they liked jocks, and the athletes got all the best-looking girls in school,

I fell short of that fact, at first, and began to hang out with some of the groups involved in gangs. They had their way with the girls as well.

These guys constantly partied and hung out with really no vision for the future.

At that time, I had no clue about my future, either, and I really didn't care at the time.

All I knew, was I *thought* I was hanging out with people who were my friends. It was fun at the time.

We would ditch school and go to friends of friends' homes and just idle around most of the day.

I knew all the gang names, White fence, 1st Flats, Big Hazard, Little Hazard boys, Evergreen, Little Evergreen Dukes, the Black Panthers, and the Chicano movement at the time was called La Raza,

I had friends in these gangs, not ever becoming a member with any of them.

But these gangs gave me a sense of worth, like being a part of a family, sort of.

It's a myth that gangs help kids find a family they never had. Gangs are involved in criminal activity with lots of violence and most of their members end up in prison or dead.

Do not confuse them with positive role models such as surrogate parents or families.

I remember the school hallways constantly being full of students just hanging out by the lockers, guys talking with girls, and vice versa.

I remember at the time, the style of dress was an Ivy league kind of look, plaid shirts, short sleeves, slacks with a cuff, and wingtips.

That was cool, but of course, being as poor as we were, I didn't have it, so I worked for it, I would cut grass in the neighborhood to earn money so I could buy those things.

I noticed all the guys were combing their hair back, instead of parting it on the side, which I did, too.

When I started to comb my hair back, my mother would get angry with me at times, because I had to use her hairspray to hold it in place!

But I was looking *good.*

A junior high kind of guy.

As time went by, a more relaxed look came into play, it was the original 501 Levi's Button Fly Jeans, with a cuff at the bottom, and white Converse basketball shoes.

Those were the days.

For P.E. class we would be outside in the yard involved in all kinds of activities, just hanging out with other students.

Most of our yard was blacktop, we had very little grass in the area.

That's how it was in the inner city and ghetto areas of LA.

All the things that I was involved in while attending junior high, no one knew about, because no one was home, it was just me and my mother.

I had no supervision.

I was running wild. My brother and sisters were gone by this time. I was functioning like an only child.

Many times, I felt like an ass, not really giving my mother a hard time, just not being a good son, and I felt guilty about it much of the time.

I guess that's why I never really got involved with the gangs, out of respect for my mother.

She did talk to me at times and told me that those friends that I had were not good enough to be around and that if I kept it up, I would end up in a bad place while attending Hollenbeck Junior High,

So, I began to get more involved in sports, I was part of the baseball team, along with basketball and football,

In my last year in junior high, I finally began getting my act together, I started to be more open and sought the counsel of my teachers.

It was a wise move.

They knew I was having problems with my studies, and not really a member of the Good Student Program.

You could say that I accepted that I wasn't a smart kid, and this was how my life was destined to be. I would sit in class when it came to reading things aloud.

I was scared to death.

Other students would read and have no problems, but when the teachers would ask me to read, I would get so nervous I could feel my body overheating out of fear.

I couldn't read a sentence because I would get very nervous to *read* a word aloud knowing that it would make me look foolish.

I was terrified that I would be made fun of in class. It wasn't that I couldn't read, I just couldn't do it in front of people.

In fact, because I felt so powerless, I would just give up. I had no help, and it would tick me off at times when others made fun of me.

I just wanted to physically rearrange faces on some of those students, not all of them, just the ones that singled me out for having that problem.

But some of the teachers would pull me aside or keep me after class and assure me,

"You're not lacking in brains, Richard, you just need someone to help you with your studies and have the confidence to express yourself in front of others!"

I had no one, so they helped me as much as they could, as time went on, things began to get better.

The rest was up to me.

As I got closer to leaving Hollenbeck after three years and prepared for high school, I started to realize that this was going to take a lot of work to be a somewhat decent student.

It was going to take more than just hanging out with my friends and the kids on the block that were simply satisfied with hanging with the "in" crowd.

I couldn't afford to emulate their way of life. They were lazy with no goals or drive to excel.

I started to listen to my teachers and began hanging out with those that were playing sports, I kept hearing from some of the teachers that would constantly remind me,

"You can do and be anything you want; you just have to work hard and don't ever quit! Don't ever let someone that you can't do it, Richard."

They were giving me the same mantra my mother had been pounding into me for years.

Over the summer, I worked some small jobs to help my mom in any way I could. Everything I earned went to my mother.

I worked at places like Chicken Delight, which was like El Pollo Loco, but it also served burgers and fries, sandwiches, and lots of other things.

My friends would come after practice to order things and would ask me to throw in some extra stuff, which I did at times.

Pleasing them made me feel like a VIP.

I also worked at the iconic Farmers Market on Fairfax near CBS. I would work as a busboy, cleaning tables and picking up tips.

The hours were mostly at night and I took the bus into town.

I was working my tail off at a young age and I had lots of time to think about moving up to high school.

At a very young age, I learned to provide for myself.

Although my mother did everything in her power to provide for her family, it was hard for her at times. So, I took it upon myself to try and make it a little easier for her.

I took a paper route and started delivery to some of the homes in my area.

My mother would help me fold the newspapers and then I would put them into the canvas pouch that was strapped to my bike and set out very early in the morning.

I also worked on weekends with friends and their families picking in the fields. Later in the afternoon, we would return home after working in the hot sun all day and we would be paid $5.00 for the weekend.

I would do my homework on my breaks and eat snacks they provided for us. All of what I earned here went *straight* to my mom.

I was a bit nervous of course, but it was time. I was becoming a young adult and I needed to step up to the challenge.

I was ready.

CHAPTER THREE

HIGH SCHOOL USA!

"**L**et's face it. No kid in high school feels as though they fit in.**"** Stephen King

After summer vacation, I began my high school career at Theodore Roosevelt High, home of the Rough Riders.

The first day was a *madhouse!*

There were students running all over the place, looking for their classes.

The first-time students were clueless, unlike the returning students that knew exactly where they were.

It was funny watching so many kids trying to unsuccessfully open their assigned lockers.

I never heard so many curse words in my life!

Back then, you had to share space with someone, and we were told to limit our lockers with books only, no personal stuff.

I remember it was a hot day and I was just trying to find my way around, I had a few friends from junior high that would try to orient me.

I was impressed with the history and pictures of past students who went on to become superstars in sports.

I thought to myself, "It would be cool if *my* picture made it up there someday!"

I was still very shy and not comfortable in a classroom setting due to my lack of education.

To protect me, I rushed to my classes so that I could find a seat in the *back* of the room so the teacher would not call on me.

I tried to join those students that would sit at the back of the class that was usually lacking in self-esteem.

Unfortunately, in every class I attended all *those* seats were taken.

The only seats that were available were in the front of the class, which is what I didn't want. I was scared to death of sitting up there.

The teachers would always pick someone in the front to read from our books to the rest of the class.

It wasn't too bad, I guess my teachers knew that I was nervous, and they didn't want to make me feel bad.

For the next two years, I kept to myself.

I had friends that I would briefly greet throughout the day, not really getting too involved with any of them.

My focus was to *hurry* home and help my mother in any way possible.

I also found my new love,

Music.

The songs and groups from 1969-71 were arguably the greatest sounds in entertainment history and I was totally enveloped in all of it.

Barry Gordy and Motown were my music nation. I loved all those groups, from The Temptations to The Supremes and many more.

What a great SOUND!

My personal favorite was Gladys Knight and the Pips. They permeated my soul like no other music.

Plus, I loved dancing to their rhythm.

Soul Train and Midnight Special were my "go-to" TV shows. I would watch the dancers for hours. Those young adults knew how to *move!*

That's how I learned all the steps. That was a big deal with a teenager growing up.

Credence Clearwater Revival rocked my world. They were like a military band with their pounding beats and gritty voices.

"Fortunate Son," "Proud Mary" and *"Bad Moon Rising"* brought out the gritty side of sound.

I loved them.

Definitions could never capture the talent of The Jackson Five, Santana, Edwin Hawkins and Rare Earth, unique groups that satisfied my musical tastes.

I liked my music substantive and tough.

It bolstered me for those moments when I needed to stand up for myself.

I also adored sports and growing up near Los Angeles was heaven for athletics.

We had the Dodgers, the Lakers, UCLA basketball, and USC football. It was a golden age of great players, great teams, and great moments!

The Dodgers won the World Series in 1959, 1963, and 1965. The Lakers set an NBA record for the most wins and won the championship in 1972. USC won the National Championship in 1972, 1974, and 1978, and beginning in 1964, UCLA won titles eight times in 10 years!

My favorite team was the LA Rams, and I am ecstatic that in 2022 they WON the Super Bowl!

What a great city for sports.

I was also learning to be empowered, as well.

One day in the lunch line, a bully tried to cut in line in front of me and I blocked him.

He threatened me and I stood my ground.

I was prepared for a bloody confrontation and for a while there it seemed inevitable.

But then, he backed off and left me alone. He also didn't cut in front of me, again.

It was a turning point in my self-confidence.

I realized that I could survive high school if I was prepared to *fight* for it.

My mom had always told me, "Son, you can accomplish anything *if* you are willing to work hard."

No one worked harder than my mother. She was talented, of course, but that wasn't the secret to her success. She had a belief system that never gave up.

This allowed her to succeed more than other entertainers who were equally gifted but less persevering.

I learned the power of *persistence* at a young age that has carried over to this day.

If I believe I can accomplish something, I will never quit until I achieve it!

If you think you can't, you won't.

Thanks, Mom.

In early 1968 while attending Hollenbeck Junior High, which was across the street from Roosevelt High. They underwent civil unrest that I witnessed first-hand.

The rebellion was on a racial level. We had riots between the Los Angeles Police Department and the National Guard over civil rights.

I remember being smack dab in the middle of it all, not as a participant, but as an observer.

It was a combination of black pride and Chicano pride, all fighting for the Civil Rights movement,

I recall the blacks shouting out phrases like, "Black Power!" The Black Panthers yelling out slogans from their group, and the Chicanos are following suit with their slogans.

There was Chicano power and La Raza, blacks wearing black berets and the Chicano wearing brown berets, and all of them getting their asses handed to them by law enforcement powers and the National Guard.

I was not actively involved with any of this myself, like other students that threw trash cans, tables, books, and anything else they could find to throw at the police.

I knew where I wanted to shine.

Athletics.

I started to get involved with sports in high school, and had some great role models in my coaches.

They really helped me a great deal and kept me on track.

After playing sports at Roosevelt and being guided by some incredibly caring people, I developed the skills and became a decent ballplayer; and made a name for myself.

I transferred from Roosevelt to Nogales High school for my senior year.

It was there I participated in varsity football and baseball. I lettered in all the sports I participated in and was told by my coaches that I had the *talent* to go places.

I think I knew that, but for whatever reason, I just didn't see myself making it, not saying I wouldn't have loved to.

I really didn't think I was all that great, but my coaches saw something in me that I didn't.

Deep down inside, I felt I had something more to do, something that was bigger than just sports.

At the time I was not sure what that was, I just knew it was something I had to find within myself.

Upon leaving Nogales High school, I didn't do much. I was basically just wasting my time away joining the list of ex-students that just wanted to go to school and then leave it.

Kids from affluent homes had a great support system and had a plan for their future, and those that didn't come from that kind of family fell back and spun around in circles.

I lacked the ability to figure out who I was and how to be better at life.

I had no one at home for support, or to provide guidance for a *future.*

My path to success would not come easy, and at times I felt it would never come. Mr. Jimenez and his family changed that.

"Thank you, Pop's!"

But I always remembered what Ernie Rodriquez, one of my coaches, said to me, "NEVER QUIT!" You have the talent to do whatever you want to do and be."

I had been happy growing up because I was naïve about a lot of things.

I thought most kids were poor, most kids ate unhealthily, and most kids hated school, so I was normal.

It wasn't until years later that I realized I had a tough childhood.

I was sheltered by a great mom and the families of Munoz and Jimenez.

They were the keys to surviving East LA.

As I neared the age of 18, I had no idea of the future that lay before me. I can't say I was ready for it because it was a fog bank of uncertainty.

The magic bubble of high school had burst and now I was on my own to face an adult world that would test me as a man.

Would I succeed or fail?

One way or the other, I would find out the answer.

So, a year after leaving school, I broke out of my doldrums and tried to figure out what I was going to do with my life.

I decided it was time for me to serve my country.

So, I did.

CHAPTER FOUR

THE PATRIOT

"**America without its soldiers would be like God without His angels.**"

I love my country. I would give my life for it.

We are the greatest nation on earth, and I believe it is the duty of every citizen to give back to America in any way we can. I was willing to make any sacrifice I could to proudly honor the United States of America.

My first duty station was basic training at Fort Ord, California, near Monterey.

Here, I would spend the next eight weeks learning the basic skills of becoming a soldier and the fundamentals of military life.

Basic training was not for intellectuals or free spirits.

You strictly followed the regimen and never questioned anything. You marched, you chanted, you ate, and you pooped.

Then, you slept and you marched some more.

That's it.

You have no life of your own.

During that time drill sergeants were still allowed to put their hands on you. Not only did they yell and scream in your face, but they were also allowed to get physical with you, as well.

Back then, this was the standard, and in an all-male basic training they would have us in formation, sometimes dressed, sometimes half-dressed. In the cold, heat, day or night.

One of the worst things I remember about basic training was that they made you dry shave in ranks, this could be very painful for some.

Not me, I was still young enough to never shave, my face was still smooth like a baby's butt!

But that didn't stop the drill sergeants from making *all* of us shave. I was lucky with no hair on my face yet.

Here I would receive my first military meal.

When it came to grub, you could not pick and choose what you wanted, it was eat or starve.

Of course, Uncle Sam wanted the best for us, so they fed us the famous S.O.S. meal, which stood for "SHIT ON A SHINGLE".

It was white gravy with what appeared to be unknown meat in it. It came with vegetables, a roll, and a piece of fruit.

It was disgusting at first when you looked at it, but eating it wasn't so bad. It's amazing what you eat when you are hungry!

I had no problem with that kind of diet after growing up on unhealthy foods all my life!

During those eight weeks, we did nothing but run, and run some more, do pushups, chin-ups, sit-ups, and a lot of yelling!

It got so bad for some of those guys who had never been away from home that we would hear them crying in their bunks at night.

They were out of luck, they couldn't just quit, they were under contract now, and Uncle Sam owned their ass.

They are part of the Green Machine now.

After completing basic, I was reassigned to Fort Gordon, Georgia. I was assigned as a communications operator.

There, I would learn the areas of a CO from the switchboard, field wiring, and telephone operations.

Some of the training that I received was laying telephone lines from telephone poles and learning the military codes, along with laying down the wire from our CP. (Command Post) to other units in the field so that we were able to communicate with one another.

Communications are far more advanced now.

This job was very difficult at times, due to the weather.

It could be pouring rain at times, or cold as hell, and in humid Georgia, unbearably hot!

But it had to get done because the units depended on me.

I later took on a secondary MOS as an infantryman with 11 Bravo.

After completing my four weeks of training as a communications operator, I was reassigned to airborne school (jump school).

So, with two MOS's 11 Bravo (Infantryman) and 36K2P (Communications Operator) the "P" stands for paratrooper.

My new duty station will now be in Fort Benning, Georgia, home of the Army's iconic Airborne Paratrooper School.

This training was usually three weeks long, and if you were unlucky, you would get there one week early, which was what we called "Hell Week!"

And yes, I was unlucky.

In time, you would do nothing but physical conditioning and run from sunup to sundown.

Every time you stepped out of a building you were required to *run* to your next destination.

If you were caught walking, you were defying the state of Georgia.

After Hell week you began jump school and started running like a mad fool, again.

Week one was ground week, accompanied by the legacy of transforming soldiers, marines, airmen, and sailors into sky warriors and becoming the next generation of airborne paratroopers.

Before starting the course, students had to complete a physical test to make sure they were suitable for the training.

They would have to complete a physical abilities test, which included pushups, sit-ups, and a two-mile run. Which ended up being three times that.

It may sound easy, and it should be, but they weeded out about 50-60% of the students that first seven days.

After that they moved you to parachute training which included packing your chute, handling the harness, and exiting the mock doors of the jump plane.

Here you learn how to exit the aircraft and properly execute the landing or, PLF, parachute landing fall.

If we succeeded in-ground week, we then train on the 34-foot mock towers.

34 feet may not sound high, but if you have never been that high before, it can be scary to most people, and you wouldn't believe how many legs don't complete that exercise.

In week two, we moved on to tower week. We continued to learn the basics of becoming a paratrooper on the 250-foot towers.

If you think 34 feet high, 250 feet in the air on a harness will scare the shit out of you!

If you have never been that high, they often send you back for more training on the suspended harness and the swing lading trainer apparatus, which includes mock doors and landing techniques, and more than 34-foot towers.

This training was a graded exercise, and you must pass it to move on to the higher elevation.

At 250 feet on a harness with a parachute, you could literally see the state of Georgia.

What a sight!

But you didn't have time to enjoy the view, it was time to JUMP!

As you fell to the ground and prepared to land, you had an instructor at the bottom yelling instructions at you on a megaphone telling you what slip to pull, so you didn't send yourself into the tower!

If you succeed here, you move on to jump week.

In week three, you were qualified to *experience* jumping out of a plane.

That was the week we all looked forward to following the initial steps of training.

You *think* you are ready at this point, but you still have some reservations about succeeding here.

Believe it or not, people go through this training and abruptly walk away from it on the tarmac.

In fact, the guy in front of me walked away just before getting on the bird, and I almost followed him.

Here you make five jumps to qualify and get your wings, two Hollywood jumps with the basic equipment, two jumps with all your combat gear, and a one-night jump with combat gear.

During that time, the "pucker" factor kicks in and your adrenaline is at its all-time high.

Not everyone can jump out of an imperfect aircraft, but those who do, are part of a lifelong brotherhood of bad-ass paratroopers!

And those that are not, will be LEGS for the rest of their lives.

After my completion in jump school, I can tell you that this course was very *demanding*, physically and mentally, and during this whole process, I was getting my butt kicked every which way, and there was no room for those that were weak and couldn't handle it.

We had a special saying in jump school when you felt that you were about to break, "take two salt tablets, a sledgehammer, and drive on troop."

I was reassigned to attend Army sniper school, located at Fort Benning. This was a three-week course.

I had to undergo three phases to complete the course. If I did not pass one of them, I was done.

The purpose of this course was to educate snipers to be adaptive soldiers, critical and creative thinkers, armed with the technical, tactical, and logistical skills necessary to serve successfully at the sniper team level.

It prepared snipers with a principal understanding of team duties and responsibilities.

The scope of the course was to teach and train the basic/advanced skills of selected individuals assigned to sniper positions to deliver long-range precision fire and collection of battlefield information.

I received training in fieldcraft skills; advanced camouflage techniques, concealed movement, target detection, range estimation, and terrain utilization (macro and micro), intelligence preparation of the battlefield (IPB), relevant reporting procedures, sniper tactics, and advanced marksmanship.

The latter was known for unknown distance firing at stationary and moving targets during daylight and limited visibility in varying weather conditions and staff subjects (intelligence, mission, training, combat orders, command, control, and training management).

Whew!

A lot of *complicated* stuff.

But it was designed as professional protection for sniper survival. This is big-time, folks.

All those areas would help me to ensure that the mission would be accomplished without *compromise* in accordance with the supporting units involved.

One of the weapons of choice in the early 1970s was the Springfield M1 Grand, which is the weapon I was trained with at sniper school but was later replaced with a Springfield M14 rifle, a 7.62mm NATO (.308 in) ammunition, which was later replaced by an M16 rifle in mid-1970s.

Technological upgrading was necessary to equip a sniper with the necessary tools to do my job and live to talk about it.

My next assignment was at Fort Bragg in Fayetteville, North Carolina. It is the home of the famed 82nd Airborne Division.

Here I would take on another course in advanced marksmanship (a sniper course).

While there, we as service members looked forward to hitting the town and clubs, and believe you and me, they knew we were coming!

We visited Rick's lounge, Prince Charles, Town pump, and the Skyline, which was on the very top floor of the tallest building in the city.

Another of our favorite haunts was Cherry Point located near a Marine base that was within driving distance of us.

The Marines would frequent the town of Fayetteville, which is *army* country and home to the famed 82nd Airborne Division and the 5th Special forces group.

So, when the Marines visited our turf, they would flex their pride, which was fine, because we would do the same.

We would drink and shout our slogans out to each other, but at the end of the night, we would be sitting at the same tables drinking and just having a good time.

We all knew that we were all on the *same* team with one purpose and that was to defend this great nation.

This is what patriots do. They all come together to serve Lady Liberty.

I don't really care what branch of service or what unit you served, you are all my brothers and sisters, and I would be willing to give my life to you.

From the moment you put on a uniform of a military member, be a first responder or in the medical field, you have all earned the title of American heroes.

You have all chosen to do the difficult jobs that others will not take on.

God Bless the United States and her fighting men and women! In uniform.

I went on to complete many other military schools to advance my skills in jungle warfare.

This was a bad time in our country with the Vietnam war continuing to escalate.

There were rumors it was coming to an end, but if not, I would be headed to Southeast Asia.

I was prepared as a soldier in every sense of the word. Now, it was up to the politicians to decide if my presence in Vietnam was needed.

CHAPTER FIVE

RETURNING HOME

"**You can't go home again.**" Thomas Wolfe

Following my end of the tour of service, my return home was not so pleasant.

It was not what I was expecting from a vet when he came home from serving his country.

As I was waiting to board my flight at Piedmont Airport in North Carolina, I was approached by two gentlemen who already knew my name.

I thought maybe they were friends of some of my friends in the unit, but that wasn't it at all.

They had all the information on me and the schools that I had attended while serving in the military.

After talking with them for a few minutes, I started to put the picture together.

These guys were contractors that worked in the private industry as mercenaries, and they were trying to *recruit* me as an operator.

I thought at first, "This would be cool!"

The money was good at the time. Back in those days, contractors would get paid up to $10.000 a tour.

In the 70s, that was a lot of money!

They mentioned my infantry training along with my experience in parachuting and sniper experience.

It all sounded good, but my focus that day was to go home and nothing else.

I told these two guys no thanks, at that point my family was everything. Long after leaving the military I would get involved with Government contract work.

There was really nothing else that came close to it.

The greatest emotional need of a person is to love and be loved.

I believed the greatest need of a man or woman was to form an inseparable connection with another member in uniform.

In the military, we made strong bonds with friends that we met along the way. Many of those new friends would always be family to me and would remain my brothers for life.

I would always cherish the time we spent together because they were my battle brothers and would forever remain in my heart.

Unless you have had that experience, you could never comprehend what I was talking about until you had lived it.

On my flight home, I thought about the memories that I had shared with those I had met in the military, some good and some bad.

Hanging out with my brothers, the good ones, knowing that they would have *given* their lives for me and me for them, sharing our backgrounds, working together, and helping one another in time of need, was *priceless.*

They say that you meet your best friends in the military, this I can say was a classic truism.

When we went to school, we met new friends in class and in the hallways or playing fields and had a connection during our teenage years, that was special.

But in the military, it went to a whole different *level!*

There, we were talking about life and death.

My brothers in the barracks or during the training would always have my back and me theirs, and we would carry this with us for the rest of our lives.

If you come across a military member or a first responder, it would be a nice gesture to buy them a cup of coffee or a meal.

But I can say from experience that a simple thank you was all they really wanted.

Just let them know that you were thankful for their service.

There was ample gratitude for them.

While on my flight home, I was treated nicely in uniform, looking sharp in my Cochran jump boots as if they looked like glass with the spit shine on them, which was a tradition in the airborne world.

And, feeling like a stud, I was proud to have served the United States of America.

Everyone on board was so kind, buying me drinks and thanking me for my service to our country.

It made me feel great to be an American!

After landing at LAX International, I gathered my duffle bag and started to walk to the door that led out to the street to wait for my sister to pick me up.

I was so excited to be home, for this was to be a surprise for my mother, who had *no* idea that I was returning to her.

While I was standing on the curb, a man behind me came up and snatched my beret off my head and began calling me a baby killer, a rapist, and all sorts of other names.

This guy looked just like the idiots we were reading about who ran to Canada and refused to serve their country.

He was a long-haired, hippy-looking SOB who had no idea he was about to have his face and ass rearranged in a split second to act like the ass wipe that he was.

I believe in the Constitution, and I fully understand the Bill of Rights and the First Amendment.

We were a free country, and everyone was entitled to their personal opinions, no matter how obnoxious or rude.

But I was also entitled to *my* opinions, too.

I had the right to serve my country and make all the sacrifices necessary to preserve our freedoms.

To have a hippie punk demean my contribution just because he didn't agree with it, needed to be addressed.

It was ironic that I had served in the military to preserve this mutant's right to bad mouth his country and me.

As I put my duffle bag down and prepared to become his worst nightmare, I happened to look past him and saw an L.A.P.D. patrol officer sitting in his black and white.

I raised my arms to the side and made a gesture to the officer and gave him a look like, "You better do something, or this idiot was not going to survive the night!"

The officer exited his vehicle and approached the subject from behind and took him down to the ground.

After the officer neutralized the POS, I overheard the people that were standing around the incident, old and young, male and female, who informed the officer, "The soldier did nothing wrong!"

The officer asked me if I wanted to press charges against him. I was very **upset** as you can imagine, but simply looked at the officer and stated, "Just give me my beret and get that piece of shit away from me!"

All those good things that I had heard on the flight on the way home, and the joy that accompanied them, were gone.

I was now living in a real-world of protest and hate, and unsure how to feel about being home.

I believe in the First Amendment, which gives anyone the right to demean patriotism, shame our soldiers, burn our flag, and refuse to stand for the Star-Spangled Banner.

We lived in a free country that honored all views, races, opinions, and religions. I respected it.

But I didn't have to like it.

You never imagined that you would be treated with such disrespect when you returned home from serving your country.

Then the ugly reality kicked in.

CHAPTER SIX

SIGNIFICANT MOMENTS

"We never remember facts, only moments." Cesare Pavese

The most significant moment of my life was the birth of my six beautiful and healthy children.

The joy of being a father, knowing that I have children, was an overwhelming blessing!

You can't ever top that.

All the medals and awards that a man could receive would never match the title and honor of the word, "Daddy!"

That is a title that stands above all others and would never leave you, even after you had left this wonderful world.

Here is a small message to my children, a quote I read somewhere along the way that has stayed with me and made me think of my kids whenever I read it.

Be you, a genuine original,
Find your voice and make a difference,
Don't forget where you came from,
But never lose sight of where you are going.
Believe in your gifts,
Cherish them and explore their possibilities.
Make mistakes and don't be afraid to ask questions.
Be brave and wild at heart.
Embrace all the things that make you unique.
Be passionate about the things that matter to you.
Always practice kindness and compassion.
Be a hero to someone.
Demonstrate character and be a good friend.
Become someone that you will be proud of when you look
back on your life
and remember all the quirky things
about yourself, that sometimes you wish were different,
You are really the most special because you are the real
thing!

And always remember that your daddy will always be here, and you will always be in my heart, thoughts, and prayers.

Some of the other significant moments of my life that deeply affected me began with September 11, 2001.

That was a day I will never forget.

It devastated me as a veteran who served this country so proudly to see this take place here at home.

It was gut-wrenching to me as I watched those planes smash into the Twin Towers in New York City on television.

To think that this happened to us in our own backyard!

How could this take place in the greatest country in the world and with the strongest military?

There is no excuse for this to take place unless our national leaders were asleep at the wheel.

We were sloppy with too many holes in our national security.

There was absolutely no excuse for this to take place.

Our preparations for preventing such an attack had been gutted by two presidents and their military consultants over the previous years and months before the event.

We had become soft in how we had responded to threats. We have given terrorist openings to successfully compromise us.

We still do.

Our politicians are more worried about illegals in this country as opposed to our own citizens, all for the purposes of Election Day votes and power.

Don't get me wrong here, I'm all for helping those who wish to embark on the American dream, but I am against those who wish to come here and commit crimes, break the laws, tarnish our country, and terrorize American citizens.

If you choose to embrace the American dream, do it the American way and obey our Constitution.

Feel free to come here, but if you don't respect our laws and fight for our freedoms, then stay the hell away!

It seems like our political leaders are willing to put their own citizens at risk so they can make a name for themselves and become financially wealthy in the process.

That's wrong.

Another moment in my life that jolted my senses was the JFK Assassination on November 22, 1963.

I will *never* forget it.

As a young boy, I saw this live on television with my mother, who broke down and cried as the drama unfolded.

I had never seen my mother cry in my life, until that moment.

That was traumatic for me.

I was not quite sure what was happening but to see her fall apart emotionally and in so much pain, it seared a memory in my soul.

It wasn't until I became older that I realized what had taken place that day.

Let's hope that it never takes place in our country again. To have an American President assassinated is a terrible thing to happen to a nation.

As Americans, we have the right to disagree with our leader's policies, but to have our political role model taken out is not the America I was born in.

We are better people than that, at least I thought we were.

A happier memory was the moon landing in 1969.

As a kid, I watched this on live television with my mother and other family members. It was such an amazing thing for a child to experience.

The moon!

It was history in the making, and for me to see it live with my mother was extra special.

I saw that amazing glow in her eyes. She was so proud to be an American!

Of course, I was too young to understand what she must have been feeling at the time, but I knew she was patriotically proud and that was good enough for me.

The Olympic games were a treasure trove of memorable moments for me.

These superb athletes lit up my life!

The American boxers at the 1976 U.S. Olympics that won gold medals included my all-time hero, Sugar Ray Leonard, Michael, and Leon Spinks.

Two awesome swimmers, Mark Spitz (1972 Munich Olympics) and Michael Phelps (in several Olympics), dominated the pool to my delight.

I choked up as I watched Muhammad Ali lighting the torch in Atlanta at the 1996 Olympics, and who could forget the "Miracle on Ice!" hockey team beating the Soviets 1980 at the Winter Olympics in Lake Placid, New York!

Wow.

But not all the moments were good.

On November 4, 1979, 52 patriotic Americans were taken hostage by militant students at the U.S. Embassy in Tehran, Iran.

It made me sick to my stomach.

For over a year, 444 days to be exact, I watched a politically impotent Democratic President, Jimmy Carter, bumble and fumble his way into resolving the crisis.

He failed miserably.

My heart went out to these captives and their families. As Americans, we felt powerless and angry as each rescue attempt failed to bring our brothers and sisters home.

On January 20, 1981, on the day our new President, Ronald Reagan, took office, the hostages were set free.

Of course, Jimmy Carter took credit for the resolution.

Nice try, peanut boy. We weren't buying it.

We finally had a strong leader in the White House.

In L.A. sports, the Showtime Lakers titles that I witnessed in person in the '80s, the Dodgers World Series Championship on a miraculous home run by Kirk Gibson in the 1988 World Series, which I attended, and the history of Jackie Robinson breaking the color barrier in baseball, stand out in my mind.

What do all these people have in common, you ask?

They were all American sons and daughters that answered the call for God and country to represent Lady Liberty and Old Glory who made us proud to be Americans.

They were true patriots, and we as a people need to understand how lucky we were to be born in the greatest nation on earth!

I have had some lows and highs, good and bad in my lifetime, but I will never forget how blessed I was to be an American, and I will defend her until my dying breath.

We, as a people, need to stop whining and start stepping up about the real problems that face our nation. If we don't get it together now, we will be at a point of no return.

What I mean by that is we may never be able to recover from the bad decisions our leaders have made, and America will implode from within, like Rome and Greece.

We as a people have the *right* to speak about our differences and to vote our consciences.

That's what makes us great. We are the shining star of the world, the land of freedom and democracy.

We are the envy of every other country that wants to be like us.

Remember this, when things don't go your way, and you start to act a damn fool by becoming violent because things irritate you, that does not give you the right to *destroy* a business, beat up on people, or soil our country.

The whole world is watching us, is this really the message we want to send to other countries?

I think we are better people than that, just think of how much we can accomplish if we could work *together,*

I understand why people get out of control.

From the beginning of our nation, we as a people had been told that if we vote for a party, Democrat or Republican, things would get better.

But as we all know, the only people that benefitted from this partisan political system are the rich and powerful.

Minorities in America don't have a chance.

Very few of them make it out of the inner-city, and our politicians have promised false hopes.

Don't insult my intelligence and try to convince me that it's not like that. As a child living in the inner-city and the ghetto areas of Los Angeles.

These areas - Compton, Watts, the projects, East L.A. Boyle Heights, and South Central - are like financial prisons with little or no opportunity for poor people.

As a young boy, we had nothing, and my mother struggled.

Today, almost 50 years later, these same areas remain the same with little or no change.

Families are depressed, and they can't help but to turn to crime, violence and drugs to survive.

Our government and elected officials have failed these hurting communities and so I tell my people,

"Don't keep believing in your elected officials if they do not come through on what they *promise* to, vote them out on Election Day!

<u>You</u> have that power across America.

Use it.

The government wants your votes, that's it. They have no intention of following through on their promises. They want to better their *own* lives, not yours!

Give them one chance at election time. If they don't come through for you, vote them out.

Start taking your community and your country back!

CHAPTER SEVEN

MY MOTIVATION

"**A mom is usually the greatest motivator.".**

Throughout my life I have been motivated by many people, some of the coaches, some of the family, friends, and even some that have not been part of my personal life.

First and foremost, my biggest motivation came from a person who was uneducated and could not read or write but gave me all she had.

This woman gave me the caring, the wisdom, and the greatest legacy of all…

The Gift of Life.

My mom.

She was one of the hardest-working people I ever knew.

The everyday sacrifice that my mother made for me every day of her life was beyond priceless.

Make no mistake, she was the driving force behind all her children.

Moms can be dependent on when things go wrong. They are always there to tell us when we do well and to remind us of when we do wrong.

That's their job.

Some of my motivations came from my coaches, who, at times when I was feeling like a failure, came to my rescue and let me know that beyond a single mistake here and there, I had meaning in life.

My friends and family would do the same.

One friend that I owed a lot of thanks to was my best friend while serving in the military, Rick Lozano, who retired as a First Sergeant with the 7th Special Forces Group (AIRBORNE) Bad Ass.

I met Rick while stationed at Fort Bragg, North Carolina, with the 82nd Airborne Division.

That guy was on point as a soldier in every way.

Before I met him, I was not going in the right direction as a military professional, not in a bad way, I was just not buying into the soldier mold.

He took me under his wing, he may not have known this, but I got turned around after meeting him.

Rick was a true mentor.

He took pride in his uniform, boots, and all the details it took to be a great paratrooper.

Not only was he my brother-in-arms, but he also remains my very best friend.

To date, we are still in touch with each other. He played a major role in the road I took in becoming who I am today.

Thank you, brother,

Others that have had an impact on my life would be my comrades in law enforcement, the military, professors, co-workers, and many people I have met along the way.

I have so many people to thank, even those that would not even realize how much of a part they played in my life.

Or, as William Shakespeare aptly put it,

"A friend is one that knows you as you are, understands where you have been, accepts what you have become, and still gently allows you to grow."

To my motivational friends, I say thank you as well.

All of this and so many others shaped me into becoming the man that God created me to be.

Motivation doesn't only come from famous people, it comes from every aspect of our lives and every person we meet along life's way.

It's right there in front of us, but it's up to us to see it and *embrace* it!

It's all around us, grab onto it and enjoy the ride, and be proud to be here on this majestic planet we call Earth.

America is a great country. There's no other place like it.

We are the gold standard of greatness. Many other countries despise us for our success and the freedoms we grant our citizens.

Yet they would like to be just like us, and those that do not respect us don't believe in liberty and the preciousness of life.

We are the greatest nation in the world, make no mistake about that, and that is why everyone wants to come here and meet Lady Liberty in New York Harbor.

We, as Americans, have a caring heart, and we will do all we can as a nation to help those in need. But make no mistake, if you try to hurt our citizens and country, you will pay a heavy price.

Yes, we all have things that motivate us.

For me, it is my children.

I have always wanted to do something to make my kids *proud* of their father.

I feel I have not always come through on that, but I will continue to keep trying.

Hopefully one day I will achieve that in their eyes.

When I was growing up, I had no father and no big brother around as a male role model to guide me in the right direction.

I had to find men that could fill that void in my life, the dads Jimenez and Munoz, my coaches and teachers, Rick Lozano, and several others who taught me to be a man.

And at the core of that struggle was my lovely mom who always believed I was destined to be a great human being and guided me there.

CHAPTER EIGHT

MY CHILDREN

"**The soul is healed by being with children.**" Fyodor Dostoevsky

Honestly, this is going to be a tough area for me to cover, only because I feel I have failed my kids as a parent.

I don't know why I was such an inept father, and there is no excuse for it.

No one was to blame but me.

I decided at a young age to dedicate my life to serving my country and community, and in the process, forgetting about my family.

I wish I could go back in time to correct that decision.

My first-born child, Richard, who we nicknamed "Bear" because he was so big at birth.

I was so proud to have a son!

Richard was born while I was away serving in the military and stationed at Fort Bragg which was the home of the 82nd Airborne Division, America's Guard of Honor.

I didn't see my son until almost a year after his birth, and when I did, he was afraid of me.

That was to be expected since we had no contact for twelve months.

Over time, he began to feel a little more comfortable with me. Soon, you could not keep us apart!

Every morning when I rose, my son would get up as well to discover what place we would visit together that day.

He was always ready to go with me, even if we just went outside for some air or got the mail.

Me and my Shadow.

I remember coming home from work on many occasions excited about picking him up, hearing his laugh, and holding him in my arms.

One night, I came up the stairs and entered his room. It was almost midnight. There he was in a dead sleep.

I leaned over and gave my son a kiss on his forehead, as usual. I whispered to him, "Don't worry son, your daddy isn't going anywhere!"

We were inseparable.

We got our haircuts together, shopped together, went to the batting cages, watched sports on TV, we were huge USC football fans along with the Dodgers, Lakers, and Rams.

When my son wore his Dallas Cowboys t-shirt I would give him shit about it from time to time, but he was my son, and whatever team he decided to cheer for would be fine with me.

As Bear got older, he began to play sports and started to make a name for himself.

My heart swelled with pride as he went on to play Little League baseball and Pop Warner football.

But my marriage wasn't good.

When my son turned five, things started to go south with his mother and me.

No one was to blame here.

Things just started getting harder for us, and we realized we were not compatible, so we separated and eventually divorced.

Richard took it very hard, and so did I. By then I was not as involved as I would have liked to have been, and my boy and I drifted apart.

He went on to participate in sports at the high school level and had the talent of taking it to the next level, but like his father, he became a dad at a very young age and needed to work and support his family.

He did a much better job than I had done. I was so proud of him.

I was constantly telling him, "Good job, son!"

At times, we would get together and play 18 holes of golf, and he was always trying to beat me at it, (which never happened) but he kept trying, which I expected since he had the same competitive juices as me.

I was still so very proud of Richard, even though he had the determination to keep trying to take his dad down,

When I played in a men's baseball league, he would come to my practices and cheer me on.

I had the talent to go places in athletics but never got past the semi-pro levels.

Our teams would travel to Mexico to play the teams there. I was told by my coaches while attending a high school that I had the potential to play professional baseball.

My wife and I were blessed with a second child, Stacey Marie.

When Stacey was born, I was technically still at home but emotionally phasing out of the family.

As a result, I didn't spend that much time with her.

I didn't have a strong connection with her at first, but we began to click as time went by.

Stacey was a shy little girl, full of energy, but I was not there to fulfill her needs,

Thank God for the in-laws, Mr. and Mrs. Jimenez, and Stacey's mother, who provided her with the love and care that I was unable to provide because I was no longer around.

I was brought up in a broken home and never had that father figure in my life to fill those shoes, I was the only child at home at the time with just my mother to fill the void of an absent father, brother, or anyone else to look up to as a mentor.

I'm not saying that was the sole reason for not being a good dad, but I'm sure it had something to do with my ineptitude as a parent.

It was not until I was taken in by the wonderful Jimenez family that I began to have the confidence to care deeply for others, but by then it was too late.

I was set in my ways.

She turned out to be a beautiful young lady, inside and out, and pursued something that would make her happy.

She is now a mother herself, and I'm sure she is doing a wonderful job.

Then came my daughters, Jazz Marie and Rhika Nicole.

Jazz was my first, and probably the one I most connected with. We bonded easily.

She was a joy, even though I was a weak person when it came to saying no to her and setting boundaries.

Make no mistake here, I love each one of my children *equally* and would give my life for them without even thinking about it, as I'm sure most loving parents would do.

Jazz is a very hard-working young lady who knows what she wants and won't stop until she accomplishes it.

 As she became older, she was much more of a focused driven young lady, she knew what she wanted and was willing to work for it.

I guess we could say she had the right attitude for success.

She has become a very driven young lady, who is pursuing a career in hotel management where she holds a leadership position and is looking to advance to a management position soon.

Jazz attended a local junior college to complete her degree.

She's on the right track and has made me very proud of her!

Rhika is attending Fullerton State University and is pursuing her degree in Business, which will make us very proud of her.

I'm sure she will also make me very proud of her as she embarks on her journey to success,

My last two, Aaliyah and Avery, are the ones I know the best.

Those two kiddos are the ones I have been around mostly because I lived with them longer.

Aaliyah is so full of energy, and not shy about anything!

I can remember going to Disneyland one year. We were sitting by the stage and a Reggae Band was playing music to the audience and she literally stole the show!

Aaliyah got up on stage and danced to the music, and everyone started to clap and applaud her.

The band members were kind enough to let her entertain the crowd!

She was my little girl, and a star was *born.*

Aaliyah was only four or five at the time, and she was a very bright and energetic young lady.

By junior high, at age thirteen, she began pursuing her dream of becoming an actress and started going on auditions.

With a little help from her mother and family, she had the support and talent genes that will help her succeed on stage someday.

Or any other career that she takes on.

At times she speaks her mind.

She has a very strong personality, and she needs to be reminded at times that she still lives at home.

My youngest son, Avery, is a handful!

He is fifteen going on sixteen years old and is a big kid, who eats like an *adult.*

That little dude was always hungry!

Avery has a strong personality and is involved in community sports in his area. I have no doubt he will be great at whatever he chooses to pursue in life.

I look forward to being there with my son and I support him in every way I can as his father.

To see him grow into a young man, and later as a man in life, my son has *already* made me very proud of him.

I will continue to do so as his journey continues in life.

He has given me a second chance at fatherhood and who knows, maybe I can get it right this time!

What they're doing now.

Richard is now in the real estate business as a loan officer and is doing very well.

Stacey is happy and productive pursuing a myriad of projects. I am so proud of her.

Jazz is in the hotel industry and has just been promoted as a manager to the staff and is looking forward to more responsibility.

Rheka is a very business-minded person. She just transferred to Cal- State University at Fullerton to pursue a degree in Business.

Aaliyah is currently a senior in high school and would like to pursue a career in law enforcement with hopes of becoming an FBI agent one day.

I wonder where she got that from!

She had several offers from a number of universities in the area to see the one that fits best for her.

Avery has expressed to me that he would one day like to serve his country one day but is still at a young age to make any plans on what path to take.

I'm sure that he will make all of us very proud of whatever he chooses.

"Tragedy is a tool for the living to gain wisdom, not a guide by which to live." Robert F. Kennedy, Presidential Campaign of 1968.

I have witnessed many things, both as a kid growing up and as an adult, crime, murder, stealing, drugs, gangs, and much more.

These are things I saw while growing up in inner-city projects in Los Angeles. They are visual experiences that can never be wiped from my mind.

Was it a struggle?

Yes, of course.

But had I allowed those painful eyesores and the people that accompanied them to succeed with what they were trying to do, they would have scarred my life and I was having none of it!

Here are a few examples.

In the early 1960s, as a young child, I was surrounded by things that were going on around me in my dysfunctional neighborhood saturated with African Americans and Hispanics.

Those were the people I spent most of my time within the early 60s.

To counterbalance their negativity, I followed a young man named Cassius Clay, who went on to become Muhammed Ali, the greatest boxer of all time.

He not only lit up the world with charisma, but he was also filled with wisdom and positive energy to inspire young people like me.

At the same time, I was influenced by a man who gave me hope in that decade. This powerful leader spoke words that permeated my soul, and I have never forgotten how he made me feel about my life and my views on racial tolerance.

I am talking about Dr. Marin Luther King Jr.

Oh, how I wish this man was still with us.

In California, there was a man who began a movement that would shake up things in fields and farms across the state.

His name was Cesar Chavez.

I worked picking fruits and vegetables during that time as a young boy. I remember getting up early at 5:00 a.m. on weekends and riding to the fields with friends and their families to toil in the hot sun.

My salary was $5.00 for the weekend. But it was a decent wage for hard work well done.

I witnessed many things that would be considered racism today, but back then people just accepted it. It was a part of life.

I remember The Black Panther Party and the Hispanic group calling themselves Chicano Power "La Raza" in 1963.

I remember watching civil rights events on television with my mother, like The Congress of Racial Equality March in Washington D.C.

I admired the courage of the protesters as they stood up for minorities and bravely inspired all of us to respect diversity in our nation.

I sadly recall the four little black girls killed in a bomb blast at a Birmingham church in 1963, by the Ku Klux Klan.

Of course, I also witnessed the assassination of JFK that same year on TV.

What a loss for our country.

Five years later, I witnessed The Poor People's March in June of 1968 in Washington D.C.

The battle for integration and equal rights for minorities was a long and bloody siege filled with ongoing violence.

That was the same year that Dr. King and Senator Robert Kennedy were assassinated along with the devastating Tet Offensive, ending our hopes that we could win the Vietnam conflict.

I went on to witness many more things in my life as I got older. The historic moon landing and the horrific Manson Family murders in 1969.

One was a giant step for mankind and the other was a shameful exercise in pure evil.

A year later brought us, even more, horror at the Kent State shootings in Ohio, and as the 1970s rolled along we ended the Vietnam War, endured Watergate and the fall of President Nixon.

I saw two assassination attempts on President Ford and was sickened by the Jonestown Massacre of over 900 people in Guyana.

Dear Lord!

It seemed like every year was a tragedy.

As an adult, I was saddened and felt powerless by the Iran Hostage Crisis, shocked and stunned by the Challenger and the Columbia shuttle explosions, was repulsed by our government over the top strategy in Waco, cried at the loss of innocent children in the Oklahoma City bombing, and was left in total disbelief at the abrupt death of Princess Diana.

The Columbine shootings of two heartless teenage boys left me shaking my head.

Hurricane Katrina and the devastating flooding that swallowed up New Orleans and the use of commercial airliners as military weapons enraged me as the tragedy of 9/11 unfolded.

We live in the greatest country in the world, but we have been pounded by evil.

And, like you, I have seen it all in my lifetime.

As a patrol supervisor, I had to manage all the different personalities of my patrol officers and make sure that I was always there for them along with making sure they would be *safe* throughout their shifts.

CHAPTER NINE
THE POLICE OFFICER

"**P**olice officers put the badge on every morning, not knowing for sure if they'll come home at night to take it off." Tom Cotton

The thought of becoming a police officer began at a very young age.

It began in the ghetto inter-city area of Boyle Heights, better known as East L.A.

The first time that I had any contact with law enforcement was at our local theater on Brooklyn Avenue while sitting in my chair waiting for the movie to begin.

I saw a group of men come down the aisle of the theater dressed in tan uniforms along with their leader, a man in a dark blue uniform.

They were recruiting for the Los Angeles Police Department (LAPD).

Of course, I was too young at the time to enlist, but that memory stayed with me until I reached adulthood.

So, after I was honorably discharged from the military, I began the journey of becoming a police officer.

First, I attended a police reserve academy and became a level one reserve officer for a local agency.

Then, in 1984, I attended a full-time academy and became a fully sworn police officer with three municipal agencies.

I completed my career with a federal police agency as a patrol supervisor Watch Commander, which lasted in total 22 plus years of dedicated service to Law Enforcement.

So, after I was honorably discharged from the military, I began the journey of becoming a police officer.

First, I attended a police academy and became a reserve officer for a local agency. Then, in 1984, I became a fully sworn police officer with a municipal agency.

I completed my career with a federal police agency as a patrol supervisor Watch Commander, which lasted 22 plus years of dedicated service.

My career in law enforcement began in June of 1997 when I enrolled in a reserve police academy at one of the local colleges that provided this seminar.

I completed the five-month course and finished in the top thirty percent of my class. Upon completion, I went to work for a local police department as a reserve police officer.

I needed to complete another course to become a Level One reserve which gave me the same status as a sworn police officer allowing me to patrol on my own.

I also took on another job at a local college as one of their part-time police officers.

I worked there until 1981 when I attended a full-time police academy and became a sworn police officer with my first agency.

I went on to work for two other agencies, one of which was in Northern California, where I took on the job as a deputy (facility training officer) FTO.

I helped train new recruits where I took on the job of a deputy sheriff with the agency. I later took a break from service from law enforcement, but maintained all of my certifications and continued the pursuit of my college degrees,

I also worked with U.S. Marshall Services on a government contract for several years.

We provided transportation to medical and court hearings; high-priority custody held in the government system as we escorted prisoners to trials.

These were some bad dudes, and they knew how to work the system.

We would have custody holds from gang members from the Mexican Mafia, white supremacy, the Aryan Brotherhood, and many more criminal elements.

You had to be vigilant and keep an eye on them constantly, or they would manipulate you and the system.

The Perils of the Position

People don't realize it but there are two very dangerous situations facing a police officer.

The first is showing up in the middle of a domestic dispute. The inherent potential for violence between spouses is a minefield because you never know what to expect.

I responded to a call involving a dispute between a husband and wife, and as I was driving over, I was thinking, "Okay, both of these people are mad at each other for some reason, and I could be walking into a powder keg!"

I immediately called other units to meet me for backup.

As I arrived at the scene, we immediately realized that it was much more of a problem than we had expected!

The husband was bleeding from knife cuts and holding an automatic weapon in his hand because his wife had stabbed him. So, here he was, holding her at gunpoint while their children stood by and watched in horror.

This could have ended very badly.

Fortunately, I was able to talk them down and the crisis was resolved without any further bloodshed.

The other potential for violence is your basic traffic stop.

One late evening I responded to a speeding traffic call and again asked for backup.

You never know who is in the car and what they have planned for a police officer.

As I arrived on the scene, I noticed that the vehicle had multiple passengers in the vehicle and the officer was at the driver's side door collecting the information on the driver.

While he was running the driver through our criminal database system, I realized the smell of marijuana coming from inside of the vehicle.

The driver's check came back with a failure to appear. We were dealing with criminals from the get-go. We had all the occupants exit the car and conducted a search of the vehicle, and we found a .45 caliber Glock under the driver's seat and one of the back passengers had a 9mm Smith and Wesson in his waistband.

If the arresting officer had not asked for backup, who knows *what* would have transpired that night?

As a patrol supervisor, I always made it a point to always approach a call as if it were a life-threatening situation.

And always stay focused. Sloppiness can cost you your life.

I have responded to shootings, fires, accidents, 415 fights, robberies, thefts, carjacking, and loud noises disturbing the neighborhood.

I have also had a beat down on myself several times and have put some beat downs on myself.

These are just some of the things a police officer will encounter during his/her shifts that they work.

It takes a special kind of person to do this job and if and you can't deal with getting names called at you, spit on, having your ass handed to you, then this job was not for you!

I suggest you seek employment elsewhere. These patrol personnel do it when others refuse or won't do it.

As a patrol supervisor:

I would be the sergeant. In charge of the shift responsible for managing all officers on duty, which at times could be difficult, having different personalities and ethnic backgrounds.

But my crew always came together and knew the job at hand.

I can honestly say that patrol officers made me very proud of them when it came to getting the job done.

Of course, we had our minor mishaps but nothing serious. They did their jobs and I thanked them for that.

It was my job to make sure they had the tools they needed to complete the job at hand and make sure that they all made it home safely after their shifts.

That was important to me.

The absurdity of defunding the police

With what's going on in our world today with all this "woke" crap spewed by the liberal Democrats, why on earth would you want to defund the very people that will respond to your calls to help you?

These are your first responders.

When they come to assist you in your time of need, these are America's best. Let me remind you of some of the things that take place during a crisis.

 In 911, they went into the towers knowing that it could end their lives, but they heroically did it anyway.

In Orlando, Las Vegas, and Virginia Tech University, they ran into an active shooter while others were running out.

If someone breaks into your home, tries to assault you or carjack your vehicle, these are the heroes that risk their lives for you because they care.

They don't do it for the money because they don't get paid enough.

My advice to you in the future. The next time you're in need of help for fear that your life is in danger, call a politician and see how long it takes them to respond to you for help.

 If you want to defund anyone, pick any liberal Democrat.

In 2004 I started the process of becoming a federal police officer and in 2005 I was hired as a corporal traffic investigator. As time went on, I moved up in rank and took on many more roles in a leadership position.

I was later promoted to the rank of Sergeant as a patrol supervisor (Watch Commander).

I worked with some great officers there and will always be grateful for their friendship and help along the way.

I remained in that position until my retirement in 2017.

I can remember my mother always telling me to be kind to people and always help them out when I could.

That has stayed with me my entire life.

Finally.

On a couple of occasions, I can recall things that I had done to assist someone in need,

The first time was when I was working as a patrol Sgt. and having coffee at a local dinner in the city. It was customary for us to meet there before hitting the streets for duty.

I noticed that one of our officers would never come and join us. This was odd because we all liked him, and the feeling was mutual.

One day, I pulled him aside before hitting the streets and asked him, "Hey man, why don't you ever join us for coffee?"

He initially replied, "I just don't feel like it."

That answer made no sense to me, so I kept after him to tell me the real reason. As we talked in detail, he finally told me.

Finally, the truth came out.

"Man, I just can't afford it. I live too far away to travel back and forth to work and I'm saving my money for gas to get home every day after work!"

He confessed that he was sleeping in his van and going from there to work.

Well, the guys and I took care of that!

I had a spare room in my home, and since we were on the same shift, I told him that he could stay at my home during his days at work and not worry about food or a place to sleep.

I took him in and it worked out great for him.

My mother would have smiled at that!

On another occasion, I was notified by a high-ranking official and his wife that they were having a bit of a problem with their teenage daughter who was hanging around with some bad kids.

At times she would leave the house and not tell them where she was going, with whom and what time she would return.

Her parents were very concerned.

 So, I began stopping by their house to meet with them and their daughter. The parents asked me if I would be willing to talk with her to see if she would trust me with her problems.

It turned out that she felt her parents were a little overprotective with her. She was fifteen, and at the point in her life where she wanted more freedom.

I continued to stop at their home over the next few months and discovered she was also having problems in school.

She wasn't a bad student; she was just frustrated and needed some friends to help her out from time to time.

I spoke with both parents and filled them in on what their daughter was relaying to me.

The parents eased up a bit on their protective ways and allowed their daughter to be a teenager. It worked out for both sides and the following year their daughter made the honor roll and turned things around.

It was a very gratifying experience for me.

CHAPTER TEN
SECURITY TO THE STARS

"**A celebrity is a person who works hard all of their life to become well known, and then wears dark glasses to avoid being recognized.**" Fred Allen

In 1998, I decided to take on another challenge.

I knew what I wanted, I was just clueless on where to find it.

My friends called and asked if I would be interested in making some extra cash.

They were working for a company that provided executive protection to the rich and famous.

Of course, I said yes!

I needed a creative challenge with some entertainment value.

Then, I ran into an old friend named Richard. He worked for a security firm that catered to celebrities.

It sounded promising.

He put me in touch with a man named Tim, who was the CEO of a company that hired bodyguards for the rich and famous.

After a brief interview, he deemed I was qualified for the position and told me, "Be at the Beverly Wilshire Hotel at 5:30 tomorrow morning for your first assignment."

Exciting!

That was the setting for the movie, *"Pretty Woman,"* starring Richard Gere and Julia Roberts. It sits just off Rodeo Drive, the shopping mecca of the stars.

I was more than a little intrigued, to say the least!

I arrived by 5:15, which was my custom. I am a punctual person. I saw my buddy sitting at a desk and went over to him. He greeted me and handed me two coded keys for access to the elevator and the room where I would meet my client.

I waited with anticipation. I had no idea who would show up.

Soon, I heard children and then I saw an adult woman emerge with the kids in tow, and following her was my mystery client.

I sat there in stunned silence when I saw her.

It was Mariah Carey.

I immediately thought to myself, "Richard, you are an accomplished man, but this is a bit over your head!"

Okay, more than a bit.

She could not have been more gracious, "You're the new guy!"

I shook my head, "No, I'm just filling in for my friend Richard for the day."

She repeated her statement, "No, you're the new guy!"

I was not aware that my friend was being let go and I was replacing him.

I *was* the new guy!

"Uh, what do I call you, Ms. Carey?"

She laughed, "MC! That's what everyone calls me!"

Here I was chatting and laughing with the greatest female pop singer in American music history.

Surreal.

What's next, Elvis is going to rise from the dead and join us?

This was one of the greatest days of my life.

A kid from the barrio hanging out with a superstar that was taking me seriously.

We sat down and did some business and she told me her expectations concerning my job for her.

I couldn't wait to see my friends that night. "How was your day, Richard; anything exciting happens?"

"Just an average day, guys. Went to the Beverly Wilshire Hotel and hung out with Mariah Carey!"

Then I realized I had to keep her name and my time with her strictly *private.* I was a professional security man, not a star-struck groupie!

There would never be information passing from my client to any of my friends.

That was the nature of my job.

It was an honor to serve such a great lady. I had the highest respect for her.

Hobnobbing

As time went by, my client list started to grow, and I was working on every major show in Hollywood.

Life was good. After a few years of working with other companies, I decided to branch out on my own.

I created The Watch Group of L.A. My current website is:

www.thewatchgroupla.com

The life of a security specialist can be glamorous at times. But it is loaded with hidden challenges that can spell disaster if you are not resourceful enough to flex with it.

Succeeding in this business is a slippery slope. One mistake and you may be looking for another job.

Celebrities are high-maintenance and have little tolerance for ineptitude since it could mess up their career or image.

There was an incident early on when one of my client's chauffeurs had a problem getting to the location due to traffic conditions and disappeared. She had an important meeting at a studio executive's home to go over her next studio recording session.

I swung into action and secured a beautiful town car to pick her up to ensure her arrival there.

When I knocked on the door to her suite to advise her that I had secured a town car for her, she was more than a little grateful!

"How did you find a car so *fast?*" she queried breathlessly.

I could tell she was stunned and very pleased with my resourcefulness.

I smiled, "I'm your security consultant, it's what I do!"

That coup made me look good in her eyes.

That's how you impress the rich and famous.

On another occasion, Eva LaRue, a former star on CSI: Miami, was having trouble with a security guard at a prestigious awards ceremony in Hollywood.

Ms. LaRue had mistakenly left her credentials at home and the guard was not permitting her to enter the building.

Precious seconds were ticking away, and it appeared she would not be able to perform her duties as one of the presenters.

Until I showed up.

I *firmly* explained to the gatekeeper that she had made an honest mistake and needed clearance to enter. He was not having any of it, so I went over his head to his supervisor and solved the dilemma.

Ms. LaRue was allowed to enter, I made sure of that!

She thanked me profusely.

Then, there was the abusive boyfriend of one of my clients, a prominent actress.

They had been arguing and he was bullying her, insisting that she move out of her hotel suite.

I raced upstairs and confronted him, "Man, this is not *your* residence, it belongs to her! If anyone is leaving, it will be you!"

I gave him two options: you can leave on your own or through hotel security with the help of LAPD for the world to see.

Within minutes, he was gone, and she was relieved.

She gave me a big smile and I responded, "that's what you pay me for!"

While still working in Law Enforcement, I took on an additional challenge.

While working for the rich and famous, it was no different than being a cop. My clients all had different personalities, as was true of the general populace, just paying far more than any local agency.

Their demands were higher, and they expect your utmost professional standards to protect them. They also demanded my complete loyalty to always be vigilant towards them.

I remember working with one of my clients who was walking along a security rope that was leading her into a building where she was to be giving an interview.

While walking to the side and somewhat behind her, I saw a hand suddenly come out of the crowd and the person attached to it tried to grab her!

I immediately reached out and grabbed the intruder's arm and took him down. I shouted at my team to quickly move our client into the building.

The "psycho" turned out to be a paparazzi who was trying to get her attention for a photo.

How was I to know that?

So yes, both invasive types of fans are dangerous. I have had many encounters that I have had to deal with, but I can honestly say none of my clients have been hurt or injured on my watch.

I am immensely proud of that fact.

"Celebrities wear sunglasses in church. They're afraid God will recognize them and ask for their autograph!"

Here are some celebrity encounters I have experienced that were memorable for me.

Snoop Dogg

On one occasion on the movie set of "Baby Boy" north of LA, meeting him was very interesting.

This was my first protective detail with a rapper. Snoop was very low-key and friendly. He offered us non-alcoholic drinks and made certain we were comfortable.

I must admit I was blown away by his desire to serve us.

Snoop Dogg was an absolute prince of a man.

The "Godfather"

This is a story that is still unbelievable to me!

I met a man, Ed DeLeo, in the late 80s, who was a drama coach from New York and spent a lot of time in Los Angeles.

I went to see him in Hollywood to find out if I could make some cash on work as an extra.

As I entered his office, I could see that there was no one at the reception desk. I heard some voices down the hallway.

As I got closer to the voices, I noticed two young people talking with an agent who was sitting at his desk.

Shortly after the two young men left the room, I introduced myself to the agent who turned out to be the brother of Valerie Harper, or *"Rhoda,"* as we knew her on television.

I asked him if he was looking for people to do extra work. We had a very good conversation.

He asked me, "Have you ever done any acting before?"

I replied, "No."

He asked me, "Had you ever done *any* scenes or monologues?"

Again, no.

He told me to wait in the lobby for a short time while he went next door to pick up his breakfast.

After a few minutes, a scruffy-looking guy came in the door who I thought was a homeless man. I asked him, "Are you lost, or do you need some help?"

He sat down and we started a conversation.

I soon found out it was a setup.

The "homeless" man was Ed DeLeo, the renowned drama teacher, and he advised me that I had just performed my first scene and I was great!

Ed and I became friends from that point on.

And on one occasion, Ed asked me to listen in on a call he was having on the phone with a friend.

The person at the other end of the call informed Ed that he had to fly back to Italy to redo the end of the scene for a movie he had just completed.

The voice sounded very *familiar* to me but I just could not place it.

Three weeks later, Ed called me and asked if I could ride with him to meet a client at the Beverly Hills Hotel.

Upon arriving there, we stood in the lobby area waiting for his appointment.

I remember sitting on this round sofa in the center of the lobby with the elevators to my rear.

After the elevators opened and closed, I heard people greeting a person named Al and what a great job he had done on a recent film.

As I turned to my right, I realized that "Al" was one of the greatest actors of my generation.

Al Pacino!

No wonder his voice had sounded so familiar on the phone to me.

He had been mentored several years earlier by Mr. DeLeo in New York City. As Al's career grew, he and Ed remained friends over the years.

Al reached out and shook my hand and said, "It's very nice to meet you, Richard."

Yep, me and the Godfather.

How cool was that!

It turns out a few years later I ended up doing security for Al at the Kodak theater in Los Angeles when the AFI awards did a tribute to his career.

A well-deserved honor.

Aaron Spelling

I was very pleased with this detail. I was assigned to the residential protection of the Spelling family at *The Manor,* his monstrous home in Los Angeles.

It has 56,000 square feet with 14 bedrooms!

I had never been in a house that size in my life, it was like being in a hotel.

"Mr." and "Mrs." are how they liked to be addressed by the staff.

I worked the day shift at Manor, so I would see Mr. Spelling off to work and welcome him home when he returned.

We consisted of a two-man staff for our shifts.

At times I would cover some of the agents that needed days off and sometimes that meant working nights.

On one occasion I can remember Mr. calling me down the hallway to come and see him.

I thought he was going to assign me a task, but he simply gave me a hug and said, "We love you here, Richard, you're doing a great job!

I was pleasantly blown away.

I responded back, "Thank you Mr. I do enjoy working for you and your family!"

Mr. had a theater in his home and on weekends he allowed us as his staff to watch movies with them.

These were movies that had not yet been released to the public.

Of course, I was grateful for his generosity, but I never took part as a viewer. It was my job to provide security and protection to them.

I needed to stay focused on the job at hand.

Cigar Man

On several occasions, while working at the front door of Mr. Chow's restaurant on Camden Drive in Beverly Hills, I would stand out front while the paparazzi would be outside taking pictures of the stars that would dine inside.

During those times, I would be able to talk with some of them when they came out to smoke or just get some fresh air.

One night I was standing there when one of Hollywood's most famous actors stepped out for some air to smoke a cigar.

He stood about three feet from me.

We started to have a conversation and I said to him, "Sometimes, I am told that I look a little like YOU!"

He thought that was funny.

I turned with a smile and asked him if *he* ever had that problem. He looked quizzically at me and asked, "What problem?"

I responded with a smile, "Do people ever tell you that you look like *me?*"

He laughed and just shook his head.

We enjoyed the exchange and he returned to the restaurant. **Andy Garcia** was a good sport!

Working for **Brett Ratner** was a great experience, to say the least. He was the youngest studio executive that I had worked for during those protection days.

I knew of him before I started working for him because he was the man that did some of Mariah Carey's videos for her in the early events of her career.

I started working for Brett during his production of the "Rush Hour" movies with **Jackie Chan** and **Chris Tucker.**

They were a great cast and funny as hell!

Brett, Jackie, and Chris were not your typical Hollywood stars that would look down on you because you were not part of the elites in Hollywood. You could have conversations with them, which I did on many occasions because they were so down to earth.

Classy people.

Quincy Jones

On another occasion at the same restaurant, I escorted the very talented Mr. Quincy Jones from the restaurant to his vehicle.

Mr. Jones was the Producer and Director of the iconic "Thriller" videos for Michael Jackson.

He stopped to take a few pics and sign autographs. While he was doing this, he asked me, "Do you enjoy your line of work?"

Of course, I responded, "Yes!" not realizing that he was testing me. Quincy Jones was a prince, always kind and respectful to everyone, including the paparazzi.

I also provided the same security at the famous Spago Restaurant on Canon Drive in Beverly Hills that catered to the rich and famous.

John Ritter

While working there one evening we provided security for an event they were having for John Ritter, the star of the sitcom, "Three's Company."

Mr. Ritter was liked by many and was a favorite every place he went, just an incredibly nice guy!

We spoke briefly and he asked if there was anything he could do for me while I was providing security to all the guests there.

I don't get asked that too often from entertainers you are providing security for, but he was a rare breed, total class.

I worked and provided security for Osprey of London, the iconic British Luxury Brand of Diamonds, handbags and fancy wallets.

They had a store in the Beverly Hills Hotel and every year they would put on a pre-Oscars event there.

I was to be the only armed off-duty officer on staff that night, if I had ever been worried about working a detail this would be the one!

There were over 150 guests, comprised of the rich and famous, worth millions of dollars in one place and only *one* of me.

Oh, dear Lord.

The event was primed for a take down.

The famous rock band, Styx, was playing there that evening.

All the diamonds at the Oscars that night worn by presenters and winners were all rented at this event.

Several of the Styx band members offered me drinks, non-alcoholic, of course, throughout the night since I was the only armed officer there that night.

Loved being around these guys!

I worked on the American Idol telecast, providing personal security to all of the contestants from seasons 1 through 9.

In season two, I remember the Idol winner, Ruben Studdard, who rose to fame after winning that year.

He would later be nominated for a Grammy in 2003 for best Male R&B Vocal Performance for his recording of 'Superstar.'

On his way out of the Kodak Theater late in the evening, I asked Ruben, "Can I get a picture with you?"

He responded, "Absolutely!"

 Over the "Idol" years I met xix winners in the hallways of the venue just outside their dressing rooms.

I also had brief conversations with the three cast members Simon Cowell, Randy Jackson and, of course, Paula Abdul.

It was a great show and a wonderful experience!

Paula Abdul

One year, Paula Abdul was wearing a dress that was difficult for her to walk up the stairs that lead to the stage.

I could see that she was having a hard time, and no one was offering her any help, so I moved in front of her assistant and extended my hand to help her make it to the top of the stairs.

She looked up with that, "Why isn't anyone helping me?" look and took my hand until we reached the top. She smiled and said, "Thank you very much!"

Every time she saw me after that, she always said hi with a smile.

Nice lady.

Gladys Knight

On another occasion, I met a great guy named Conrad who was the driver for Miss Gladys Knight, the leader of the famed Pips.

My teenage favorite!

She was to be a guest speaker on American Idol that evening.

Conrad explained to me that Miss. Knight did not have security on the West Coast and asked if I would be interested in possibly providing it.

In a heartbeat, I said, "Yes!"

Later in the evening, when people were exiting the building, Conrad came out with Miss Gladys and her assistant and told her, "Miss Gladys, this is the guy I was telling you about!"

She introduced herself to me and I stood there in shock, remembering how she was my favorite singer in high school. I was talking with the one and only, Miss Gladys Knight!

Conrad and I remain great friends to this day and am pleased to say he is my brother.

Yes, he is!

I enjoyed working with my clients. They are always so grateful.

I have also provided security and personnel protection to its stars and Hollywood's biggest stages to include the Oscars, The choice awards, Grammy's, Golden Globe Awards, American Music Awards, MTV video and music Awards, Country Music Awards, Billboard Music Awards, American Idol, BET music and video Awards, Emmy's, Screen Actors Guild Awards to name a few.

CHAPTER ELEVEN

THE ART OF ADAPTING

"**A** true champion can adapt to anything.**"** Floyd Mayweather, Jr.

To be effective as a security consultant, one needs to wear several "hats" to prepare for all the possibilities these celebrities encounter in their lives.

Here are some of the most prominent ones.

Drug abuse

In their pressurized world of fame and fortune, it is sadly common that musicians and actors often turn to drugs to cope with their unrealistic lives.

The security consultant may have to not only discreetly rush them to a hospital but save their lives, as well.

We have lost dozens of icons such as Elvis Presley, Jim Morrison, Jimi Hendrix, Janis Joplin, and countless others who have succumbed to an overdose.

Anorexia and bulimia

Image is everything in Hollywood, especially when it comes to women and beauty. Not only is aging their enemy, but their weight can be a problem, too.

Karen Carpenter is the most notable fatality here, but she was only the tip of the iceberg when it came to starving herself to remain attractive in her own eyes.

As a consultant to the stars, I must be constantly vigilant in picking up any hints of self-destructive behaviors that threaten my clients.

Stalkers

Famous people are vulnerable to crazed fans and ex-lovers. The list is so long that it comprises the deaths of those who have been attacked by emotionally out-of-control individuals that have no boundaries when it comes to violence.

Mood swings

Celebrities can be moody with all the attention heaped upon them and the creativity inherent in their persona.

From day to day, you're not sure what person will show up when you arrive to pick them up!

They are never dull.

But one must understand basic psychology to handle their emotions, or you could find yourself out of a job with one inappropriate sentence.

The paparazzi

This is a mixed bag. As much as celebrities complain about intrusive photographers, they also encourage them at times.

In Hollywood, the saying goes, "The only thing worse than publicity is *no* publicity!"

The paparazzi can be rude, disrespectful, and necessary all at the same time.

It is my job to balance the contradictions.

There are constant logistical problems involving limos, schedules, and security concerns that must be addressed daily.

These issues are like gnats biting around your ankles, but they are solvable.

I love my work and after all these years, I am very good at it.

My mom taught me the value of always making people happy.

My current career.

I am the President and CEO of the Watch Executive Protection Group. www.thewatchgroupla.com

We are an acclaimed firm of security agents with a reputation for effective security solutions and the use of innovative technology in the protection of life and property.

We have a portfolio of completed and ongoing projects with a particular emphasis on governmental security.

Your lifestyle and or the profession you choose can sometimes dictate your everyday situation. There are times it can be risk-free and at times it can be wrought with incidents that can affect the safety of you and those around you, which can take place at any given time.

The Watch Protection Group provides peace of mind to celebrities, VIPs, business executives, government officials, dignitaries, and most anyone seeking high-end protective services.

All our agents come from backgrounds in law enforcement, military, or tactical training, and are *highly* qualified to do the job at hand.

They are required to maintain quarterly training in Executive Tactical Training Protection.

Our agents are certified in our Special Operations Tactical and Training course (S.O.T.T.).

They must possess several assets, which include communication, defensive flexibility, observational astuteness, assessment acuity, and proper judgment in all situations.

In addition to protective measures, all agents must pass a complete drug and criminal background check before they qualify for our company.

The double standard

Throughout my life, I have seen how our system works and needs a major fix when it comes to treating citizens equally.

A female officer in Minnesota discharged a weapon she thought was her taser and killed a perpetrator is now imprisoned for life.

But Alec Baldwin made a similar mistake with a blanks gun, killing a woman on a movie set and is not only walking the streets but jovially giving TV interviews!

Celebrities and politicians are in cahoots with the liberal media and continue to break our laws and get away with it.

And you wonder why our citizens don't trust our government!

As time went by, my client list started to grow and I was working on every major show in Hollywood. Life was good. After a few years of working with other companies, I decided to branch out on my own.

At times, people would ask me if working for the stars was more dangerous or difficult than working as a police officer.

I would respond truthfully, "They are *both* dangerous."

As a patrol supervisor, I had to manage all the different personalities of my patrol officer and make sure that I was always there for them, along with making sure they would be *safe* throughout their shifts,

While working for the rich and famous, it was no different than being a cop. My clients all had different personalities, as was true of the general populace, just paying far more than any local agency.

Their demands were higher, and they expect your utmost professional standards to protect them. They also demanded my complete loyalty to always be vigilant towards them.

I remember working with one of my clients who was walking along a security rope that was leading her into a building where she would be giving an interview.

While walking to the side and somewhat behind her, I saw a hand suddenly come out of the crowd and the person attached to it tried to grab her!

I immediately reached out and grabbed the intruder's arm and took him down. Then, I shouted to my team to quickly move our client into the building.

The "psycho" turned out to be a paparazzi who was trying to get her attention for a photo.

How was I to know that?

So yes, both invasive types of fans are dangerous. I have had many encounters that I have had to deal with, but I can honestly say none of my clients have been hurt or injured on my watch.

I am immensely proud of that fact.

On another occasion at the same restaurant, I escorted the very talented Mr. Quincy Jones from the restaurant to his vehicle.

Mr. Jones was the Producer and Director of the iconic "Thriller" videos for Michael Jackson.

He stopped to take a few pics and sign autographs. While he was doing this, he asked me, "Do you enjoy your line of work?"

Of course, I responded, "Yes!" not realizing that he was testing me. Quincy Jones was a prince, always kind and respectful to everyone, including the paparazzi.

I also provided the same security at the famous Spago Restaurant on Canon Drive in Beverly Hills that catered to the rich and famous.

While working there one evening we provided security for an event they were having for John Ritter, the star of the sitcom, "Three's Company."

Mr. Ritter was liked by many and was a favorite of every place he went, just an incredibly nice guy!

We spoke briefly and he asked if there was anything he could do for me while I was providing security to all the guests there.

I don't get asked that too often from entertainers you are providing security for, but it was a rare breed, total class.

I worked and provided security for Osprey of London, the iconic British Luxury Brand of Diamonds. Handbags and fancy wallets. They had a store in the Beverly Hills Hotel and every year they would put on a pre-Oscars event there.

I was to be the only armed off-duty officer on staff that night, if I had ever been worried about working a detail, this would be the one!

There were over 150 guests, comprised of the rich and famous, worth millions of dollars in one place and only *one* of me.

Oh, dear Lord.

The event was primed for a takedown.

The famous rock band, Styx, was playing there that evening. All the diamonds at the Oscars that night worn by presenters and winners were all rented at this event.

Several of the Styx band members offered me drinks, non-alco-holic, of course, throughout the night since I was the only armed officer there that night.

Loved being around those guys!

I worked on the American Idol telecast, providing personal security to all of the contestants from seasons 1 through 9.

In season two, I remember the Idol winner, Ruben Studdard, who rose to fame after winning that year. He would later be nominated for a Grammy in 2003 for best Male R&B Vocal Performance for his recording of 'Superstar.'

On his way out of the Kodak Theater late in the evening, I asked Ruben, "Can I get a picture with you?"

He responded, "Absolutely!"

Over the "Idol" years I met xix winners, in the hallways of the venue just outside their dressing rooms. I also had brief conversations with the three cast members Simon Cowell, Randy Jackson and, of course, Paula Abdul.

It was a great show and a wonderful experience!

One year, Paula Abdul was wearing a dress that was difficult for her to walk up the stairs that lead to the stage. I could see that she was having a hard time, and no one was offering her any help, so I moved in front of her assistant and extended my hand to help her make it to the top of the stairs.

She looked up with that, "Why isn't anyone helping me?" look and took my hand until we reached the top. She smiled and said, "Thank you very much!"

Every time she saw me after that, she always said hi with a smile.

Nice lady.

On another occasion, I met a great guy named Conrad who was the driver for Miss Gladys Knight, the leader of the famed Pips.

My teenage favorite!

She was to be a guest speaker on American Idol that evening.

Conrad explained to me that Miss. Knight did not have security on the West Coast and asked if I would be interested in possibly providing it.

In a heartbeat, I said, "Yes!"

Later in the evening, when people were exiting the building, Conrad came out with Miss Gladys and her assistant and told her, "Miss Gladys, this is the guy I was telling you about!"

She introduced herself to me and I stood there in shock remembering how she was my favorite singer in high school. I was talking with the one and only, Miss Gladys Knight!

Conrad and I remain great friends to this day and I am pleased to say he is my brother.

Yes, he is!

CHAPTER TWELVE
TOXIC DEMOCRATS

"I keep saying this to the Democratic Party. The reason why you're so toxic is that you've become the party of no common sense." Bill Maher

Our political system has been corrupted by the Democratic Party. There are no ifs, and, or buts about it.

The jackass is the perfect symbol for this group of thieves, liars, and con artists that use America for their own purposes.

To cleanse our way of life and "drain the swamp" as President Trump stated it, we must first identify the individuals that got rich off the system.

Let's begin with the couple that wrote the manual for political narcissism.

Bill and Hillary Clinton

These two characters arrived on the national scene in 1992 and almost immediately wacky headlines began popping up like a madcap pinball machine!

It wasn't just one scandal, it was several of them, and not coincidentally, millions of dollars began flowing into the Clinton's bank accounts.

Five years later, the wealthy Clintons made their money-making scheme legitimate in founding The Clinton Foundation, which now has assets totaling over 2 billion dollars!

Bill and Hillary began charging foreign countries millions of dollars in return for political favors using the White House as a glorified swap meet.

They were also paid up to a million dollars in speaking fees and Bill discovered he had access to pretty interns that fawned all over him.

He and his wife slept in separate bedrooms in the White House, and it became obvious that their marriage was not predicated on true love but political expediency.

To make matters darker, many of their political cronies and enemies began showing up dead. As more and more women surfaced claiming they were sexually assaulted by the President, he began scrambling to avoid impeachment.

Hillary was caught in so many lies that she had to go on "60 Minutes" and claim shamelessly, "I can't recall even one lie I have ever uttered in my lifetime."

The Clintons were the first politicians to use partisanship as a major weapon in their quest for power.

They forever stained the once noble image of statesmanship with their greed.

Al Gore

Bill Clinton's Vice-President loved to embellish the truth to make himself larger than life, from claiming he was the inspiration for Ryan O'Neal's character in "Love Story" to trying to convince the tech world he invented the internet!

Then, he went on a mission to scare the world that global warming would eventually destroy us without proven factual evidence to support his crazy claim.

Al Gore has always been interested in furthering his own career, not the prestige of The United States of America.

Barack Obama

When Obama was running for the presidency, Rudolph Giuliani termed him "a community organizer" incapable of managing America's highest office.

It was an astute judgment of a neophyte with an inauspicious voting record as an obscure Senator from Illinois.

Obama soon proved to be over his head in doing the job. He masterminded a payment to Iran for over a billion dollars, if you have forgotten, Iran is one of our most vicious enemies.

He was instrumental in forming the controversial "Black Lives Matter" organization and he is considered with being the racially divisive President in history.

Worse yet, he was ashamed of the United States and constantly apologized to our enemies for our historical actions.

It could be argued that Barack Obama favored Socialism over Capitalism and Islam over Christianity. As a shameless apologist for his own country, he weakened our position as a world power.

He and Hillary Clinton provided an opening for the emergence of the terror group ISIS, which was responsible for the deaths of thousands of innocent citizens, including Americans.

He couldn't fix inflation or the housing market (which cost Americans over 7 billion dollars in home equity) despite his promises that he would. He will go down in history as one of our worst Presidents ever, along with Jimmy Carter and Warren G. Harding.

He also chose Joe Biden as his Vice-President, paving the way for the hapless Senator from Delaware to be our lowest-rated Commander-in-Chief beginning in 2020.

Rudy Giuliani was right.

Community organizer Obama.

AOC

The politically inexperienced Bronx bartender with a little brain and a big mouth who whiffed over the three branches of government continues to embarrass herself on all subjects politically.

Her goal?

To become President someday.

Dear Lord, save our nation from that possibility.

Nancy Pelosi

Why is Ms. Pelosi so powerful in the House of Representatives?

The short answer is because she has raised hundreds of millions of dollars for the Democratic Party and it has rewarded her with legislative power.

It has nothing to do with political competence.

The #1 goal of all incumbents is to win their next election and Pelosi has enabled thousands of them to succeed so they show their gratitude and let her reign supreme as the House Speaker.

It's not only disgraceful, it has hurt our country beyond measure.

Bernie Sanders

Technically, he is an Independent, not a Democrat. But he votes Democrat and that is where this rabid Socialist endangers our freedoms.

He is so far left politically; he would make Fidel Castro proud.

Toxic Dems are everywhere, mucking up legislation, inciting violence, and stealing elections.

Adam Schiff has been caught in more lies than Kellogg's has corn flakes, **Kamala Harris** screams "racism" every time she is criticized, **Amy Klobuchar** comes across as the girl next door but in reality is an old-fashioned union adherent with 1930's policies that didn't work then and don't work today.

Cory Booker is the master of talking for hours without saying anything significant and, if you can understand *anything* **Michael Bloomberg** says, you deserve the Medal of Honor!

Politics used to be based upon cooperation in the spirit of making America Great Again. These current Democrats are as entrenched in their deceitful ways as a mule in quicksand. It's their way or the highway.

Unfortunately, they are the liberal media's darlings and are constantly enabled by the socialist journalists that protect their lies and destructive actions on every issue.

We need to sweep them out of the office and down the political toilet so we can regain our national prominence and decency.

God help us.

CHAPTER THIRTEEN

CRAZY (AND NOT SO CRAZY!) CONSPIRACY THEORIES

"**I**'m not a conspiracy theorist, I'm a conspiracy analyst.**"** Gore Vidal

Got to love the internet! If you want to research every possible conspiracy known to men, hit Google, and off you go.

Many of these theories involve our government and whether they are lying to us or not. Do I trust the powers that be?

In most cases, no.

I believe the American people have been lied to from the beginning of our republic. Let's begin with the mother of all conspiracies.

JFK Assassination

Who killed our President in 1963?

The suspects are innumerable from the simple (Oswald) to the silly (Jackie Kennedy). My logic tells me to start with who had the strongest motive and the most realistic means to pull it off.

Was it Castro?

Bitter Bay of Pigs patriots?

The Mafia?

The KGB?

The Military-Industrial Complex?

LBJ?

The CIA?

The Secret Service?

The FBI?

I dismiss all these groups acting alone because they don't make sense based upon their historical tendencies. Russia is primarily violent and aggressive with bordering nations and individuals, not entities thousands of miles away.

Fidel Castro hated Kennedy, but there is no evidence he had the means necessary to pull off a public assassination. The same is true of the embittered Bay of Pigs soldiers who believed the President had betrayed them in battle.

The Mafia hitmen did not choose targets surrounded by a major motorcade with thousands of people as potential witnesses.

The Secret Service could have killed Kennedy quietly in the White House to avoid detection, not on a major Dallas Street.

Lee Harvey Oswald held low marks as a sniper in the Marines at Camp Pendleton and was unlikely to successfully fire a kill shot.

That leaves us with three probable assassins, the Military-Industrial Complex, LBJ, and the CIA.

The Military-Industrial Complex was paranoid that Kennedy would have sabotaged their involvement in Vietnam, and they were right in assuming so.

He was not a proponent of a full-scale conflict, and he would have ruined the MIC's plans for power and financial gain had he lived. Thus, he had to be eliminated.

But to kill him in Dallas when they could have handled his demise in D.C?

The FBI under J. Edgar Hoover, whom President Johnson appointed for life, is also a possibility.

That leaves us with LBJ and the CIA.

The Vice-President was from Texas, and he had all the necessary machinery and contacts to pull off an assassination there.

Working with CIA operatives, such as Howard Hunt (who confessed on his deathbed that he was one of the masterminds of the assassination), would have made it easy for LBJ to not only gain revenge on the Kennedy brothers but become the President in the process.

Was Johnson capable of murdering a political rival?

Phillip F. Nelson, author of the book **"LBJ: The Mastermind of JFK'S ASSASSINATION,"** believes so. He contends that Johnson had eight rivals slain during his career to preserve his power.

Was the CIA capable of murdering a political enemy?

Just ask the families and associates of national leaders Ngo Dinh Diem in Vietnam and Patrice Lumumba in the Belgian Congo, among others. Assassinations were a standard operating procedure for the CIA.

Of course, no one can prove that LBJ and the CIA killed President Kennedy, but that is my most likely scenario.

If this is what happened, our beloved President was taken out by the internal workings of a hit squad orchestrated by our own government.

The chilling question remains, "If our government can kill an American President, what else are they capable of?"

The answer is, Anything!

The moon landing.

That depends on whether you believe that the heat shield upon re-entry would not incinerate the astronauts coming back into the Earth's atmosphere.

Senator Robert Kennedy Assassination. Do your homework. There were far more bullet holes in people's bodies and in the walls than he had in his gun. Also, remember that RFK's route which took him through the kitchen was altered at the last second, which afforded Sirhan a wonderful coincidence to shoot the Senator.

Bobby was killed by a gunshot *behind* his ear, which was a neat trick since Sirhan was standing to the front and right of him.

By the way, who was Robert Kennedy's main political enemy?

Lyndon Johnson wanted his Vice-President, Hubert Humphrey, to be the Democratic nominee over Kennedy for President in 1968.

Just saying.'

9/11.

This remains a major conspiracy debate to this day. Were the attacks on the Pentagon and New York City solely the work of Al-Qaeda or did they have inside help from our government?

The list of suspicious events in the past 246 years is too long to itemize here. But there have been so many events that make more sense when you apply our government's involvement in the context of their tragedies.

Pearl Harbor.

President Roosevelt wanted us to enter World War II so he could use the profits of a military machine to pull our country out of the Great Depression.

While he was meeting with two Japanese diplomats in the Oval Office, our naval base at Pearl Harbor was bombed, killing thousands of our soldiers.

Who orchestrated that attack?

Four years later, on V-J Day, we were financially stable again.

Hmm.

Dr. Martin Luther King Assassination. Was he really assassinated by a hapless drifter as he stood on the balcony of the Lorraine Motel or was the FBI and law enforcement in the South behind it?

J. Edgar Hoover hated Dr. King and had harassed him for years. Did he shed any tears upon hearing the news that the civil rights leader had been gunned down?

Speaking of civil rights, who killed the three volunteers from the north in Philadelphia, Mississippi, in 1964?

It was later revealed that James Chaney, Michael Schwerner, and Andrew Goodman, who were registering blacks to vote, were tortured and shot to death by the Ku Klux Klan, with the assistance of local law enforcement.

Yes, our *government.*

I will grant you that some conspiracy theories are false and should be dismissed. But not all of them are crazy. All I ask is that you keep your mind OPEN and stop believing everything our government says just because they say it.

As patriots, it is our duty to be vigilant and wise in protecting our freedoms. There are corrupt individuals and practices in every profession, including the government.

If you love your country, you will do your research to ensure that we never take for granted the liberty we have fought so hard to attain.

CHAPTER FOURTEEN

THE SHIFTING FACES OF THE SUPREME COURT

"We the people are the rightful masters of both the Congress and the courts, not to over-throw the Constitution, but to overthrow the men who *pervert* the Constitution." Abraham Lincoln

The most powerful branch of government in our country is the Supreme Court of the United States. It is the final authority on the Constitution and all things legal.

There is no appeal beyond the Supreme Court decision, save for an election or a new justice who can amend the law, which is exactly what happened when Donald Trump was elected President and he appointed three conservative judges to the Supreme Court, much to the dismay of the liberal Democrats.

As a result, the current Court stands at a clear majority of conservative thinking with a 6-3 judicial advantage.

The Elephant in the Living Room

The most hotly debated court case in American history, Roe vs Wade which gave abortion rights to women in 1973 and resulted in the deaths of over **62 million** aborted babies.

Think about that horrific statistic for a moment. The policies of liberal politics have wiped out the lives of babies and eliminated their chance to exist on earth. Not only a shocking statistic but a most shameful one.

With three new Conservative justices, the betting odds are that Roe vs Wade will be reversed, but it may take a few years to happen.

And that is the nature of the Supreme Court. This judicial branch is not a speedboat, it is an aircraft carrier that takes a ton of time to turn around. Eventually, the Constitution rights itself, but deliberately, not frenetically.

The main reason for this snail-like pace is that there is no key "swing votes" on the Court that dominated its historical past. It is more of a collaborative effort with liberals, moderates, and conservatives in unlikely alliances to effect change these days.

Strange bedfellows, indeed.

So, whatever your political persuasion, you will have to be more than a little patient because there are no quick fixes with the justices currently making up the current Court.

It is not a microwave mentality, more defined as a crockpot. Issues and decisions can simmer for months and years, not days. If no one dies allowing the President in power to make partisan change, conservatives in this country will eventually be thrilled to see their political agenda drastically improved in areas such as immigration, religion, the death penalty, gun rights, and, of course, abortion.

The Supreme Court is supposed to be non-partisan, but if you believe that, you have a short memory. In 2000, George W. Bush and Al Gore were both short of an electoral majority in the presidential election. The state of Florida was up for grabs and the winner of that state would occupy the White House.

The decision came down to the Supreme Court. At that time there were 5 justices appointed by Republican Presidents and 4 chosen by Democratic ones.

The Court ruled along party lines by a vote of 5-4 and Bush became our President.

Totally political.

That's why the justices on the Supreme Court are so critical in terms of political and societal influence. Whoever the president can determine is the way the vote goes. Pro-lifers, who have suffered under abortion laws for the past 49 years, now are on the brink of outlawing the murder of babies.

Finally.

That's why two Republican nominees to the Court were so hotly contested, Clarence Thomas and Brett Kavanaugh. After bitter in-fighting and sexually scandalous testimony proffered by the Democrats, both men were approved and will be instrumental in making the current Court a conservative one.

But it won't be automatic. There are several gray areas saturating the Court and there will be surprises over the next 20 years disappointing Republicans who are expecting a "rubber stamp" to seal their political agendas.

Overall, the Court is not a political surety, but a Constitutional one. First and foremost, the justices are passionate about the

Bill of Rights, the Amendments, court cases with historical precedent, and the law.

They don't exist to protect the Republican Party but to protect American citizens from perversions that threaten Constitutional law, a significant distinction here.

The two numbers, 6-3, are significant for several years to come.

Stay tuned.

CHAPTER FIFTEEN

THE RISE AND FALL OF THE MEDIA

"**Forget the politicians. The politicians are put there to give you the idea you have freedom of choice. You don't. You have no choice. You have owners. They own you. They own everything. They own all the important land, they own and control the corporations that have long since bought and paid for, the senate, the congress, the statehouses, the city halls, they got the judges in their back pocket, and they own all the big media companies, so they control all the news and the information you get to hear.**

They want more for themselves and less for everybody else. But I'll tell you what they don't want. They don't want a population of citizens capable of critical thinking. That doesn't help them." George Carlin

The U.S. press, like the U.S. government, is a corrupt and troubled institution. It fails to do what it claims to do, what it *should* do, and what society expects it to do.

The news media and the government are entwined in a vicious circle of mutual manipulation, mythmaking, and self-interest.

Journalists need crises to *dramatize* news, which allows government officials to appear as rescuers on a white steed to be responding to crises.

But far too often, the crises are manipulated fabrications.

Examples of these media charades include the Cuban Missile Crisis, the Barry Goldwater nuclear scare, Watergate, and the Mueller Report.

We were never in danger of going to war with the Soviet Union and President Kennedy and the liberals knew it.

What LBJ and the media did to Barry Goldwater in the presidential election of 1964 was shameful. For the ultra-liberal Washington Post and its two reporters, Woodward and Bernstein, in bringing down President Nixon was a farce, and the Mueller Report was an overhyped document that sadly resulted in House Democrats impeaching President Trump.

These were highly politicized journalistic hit jobs making mountains out of molehills for the purpose of partisan gain.

The institutions of media and liberal politics have become enmeshed in a web of lies that our citizens are unable to distinguish truth from fiction.

Simply put, since Watergate the media has been out of control hellbent on making and manipulating the news instead of merely reporting it.

Every new journalist entering politics today has visions of becoming the next Woodward and Bernstein. They want to be the stars of the show, not reporters humbly informing the public.

As a result, the public's confidence in the fourth estate, the media, has gradually eroded in the past forty years.

From 1973 to 1993, only Congress faltered in public esteem over the press.

This decline in confidence reflects a gnawing feeling that the news media is bellicose, unfair, confrontational, and obsessed with controlling the news, from CNN to MSNBC to the three major networks.

The media has become blind to specific issues.

Government spending and deficits continued to rise in the savings-and-loan debacle of the 1980s because the press was unable to focus on it until it became a *crisis.*

The media ignored the impending financial downfall because it had no idea how to report it. It wasn't exciting enough and too boring for the American people to comprehend.

It was too hard to explain so the press shoved it under the carpet. Then, when the savings and loan companies began to unravel, the media "romanticized" it with dramatic pictures of angry investors trying to get their money back.

It was too little, too late. The government was powerless, at that point, to fix the emergency.

If it doesn't "lead with bleed," The media's inability to report events or trends that are not crises creates problems in society.

Hurricanes and earthquakes are what editors want to report.

But when reporters try to cover "dry and boring trends slowly taking shape over time, news editors have zero ability to make them newsworthy.

So, they ignore them.

Which is fine with reporters who want to be celebrity stars in their cities.

Reuven Frank, a former president of NBC News, correctly and insightfully stated, "News is whatever the damn government *says* it is."

Therefore, what we learn about foreign news is as dramatic in pictures as our domestic news is, or no one would pay attention to it.

Local newscasts focus on amusing and entertaining stories, not news that is menacing, bland, or God forbid COMPLEX!

The real world is just not that exciting. When everyday people or events are reported on the news, you can see television sets being turned off.

The media has evolved into telling people what they want to hear, like the leader in the French Revolution who stated, "I must find out where my people are going so I can LEAD them!"

So, what is going on in the real world is the *humdrum* business of humdrum institutions.

News editors and their reporting puppets are consumed with sensationalism, shock value, and entertainment.

Keep those TV sets humming, folks.

If a report starts to lag or does not have a gripping essence to it, the news switches gears and shamelessly *amplifies* it.

Today, the news is no longer about the facts, but about the money. Ratings rule that is the bottom line. It is a shameful hour of deceit and exploitation. Its dog eat dog for survival.

That is why health care rarely excites the American people. The media has no clue how to market it so that viewers will find it riveting.

It limps along as a poor stepchild seeking an audience.

To make matters worse, the National Review's survey on the subject revealed that 80% of American citizens are *satisfied* with their health care.

That health care dog doesn't hunt!

Mix in the truth that the U.S. electorate does not trust Congress and the legislative potential to pass health care reforms wilts like a leaf in a summer breeze.

Instead, voters are prone to rejecting any politician that would increase big government to the horrors of Democratic liberals.

I love it!

Cynthia Crossen argues in her book, *"Tainted Truth: The Manipulation of Fact in America,"* which focuses on how advocates of policy positions and companies promoting products *deliberately* misuse scientific research to <u>further</u> their objectives.

Crossen writes, "More and more of the information we use to buy, elect, advise, acquit and heal has been created *not* to expand our knowledge but to sell a product or advance a cause."

A growing industry has thus developed to create the research to *legitimize* policy positions or marketing objectives.

Public policy debates now commonly revolve around competition rather than the merits of a proposal.

Much of the health care debate raged around differing estimates of the numbers of citizens without health coverage and the costs of the various proposals to cover them instead of a more balanced view which included those who did have health care.

Companies routinely use research studies to promote their agenda of products or positions, such as a biased study by Wonder bread that proclaimed "white bread won't cause you to gain weight and is nutritious."

It gets crazier, a study by the Princeton Dental Resource Center, funded by Mars, the maker of M&Ms, concluded that chocolate may *inhibit* cavities!

Yeah, and foxes invading hen houses would produce more eggs.

"Most members of the media are ill-equipped to judge a technical study," Crossen correctly points out. "Even if the science hasn't been explained or published in a U.S. journal, the media may jump on a study if it promises **entertainment** for readers or viewers. And if the media jumps, that's good enough for many Americans."

Absurd logic.

The media learned how to ask the right questions to prove their surveys, too.

In a 1992 mail-in questionnaire for Ross Perot in *TV Guide*, one question read, "Should the President have the Line-Item Veto to eliminate waste?"

Yes, 97% of respondents said.

But when the question was *reworded,* "Should the President have the Line-Item Veto, or not?" and asked of a scientifically selected random sample, only <u>57%</u> said yes!

It's no wonder why all the political media polls in the 2016 presidential election showing Hillary Clinton beating Donald Trump were way off.

The press loves polls and surveys. They're a surefire way to get publicity even if they are deliberately skewed.

"That's what surveys do," a Roper pollster says. "They basically *manufacture* news." Political scientist Lindsay Rogers, by the way, coined the word *pollster* as a pejorative takeoff of the word *huckster.*

Amen.

Concocted and inaccurate surveys and studies taint our perceptions of what is true and distort fair and balanced public policy debates.

The media's desire for drama *encourages* the distortion and corruption of public decision-making. "The media are willing victims of bad information, and to make matters worse, are now **producers** of it.

They have little interest in providing facts, they only desire to sell their brand of information."

The media should stop producing information that serves only to feed their *own* interests.

We need to urge news organizations to "establish a culture of responsibility and deliberation."

We also need to redirect the media's focus away from advertisers and that media monopoly should be broken up.

But the deadly combination of rapidly advancing technology and viewer apathy is dooming us as responsible, informed citizens.

With hundreds of cable channels available today, Americans are overwhelmed with deceit, distortions, and lies from the media.

For many years to come, businesses are likely to need more corporate propagandists, not fewer. We will be seeing and believing more misrepresentations from our disgraceful media.

Believe it.

CHAPTER SIXTEEN

HOW ARE WE DOING, AMERICA?

"The greatness of America lies not in being more enlightened than any other nation, but rather in her ability to repair her faults." Alexis de Tocqueville

America has always been the greatest nation on earth. Not because we have always been perfect but because we have worked hard on fixing our faults and setbacks. We have been flawed at times, but we are not a flawed country.

Here is a review of where we are at today and what we must do to overcome our shortcomings and make America Great Again!

Individual and human rights

In 2019, the United States continued to move *backward* on rights. According to the liberal Democrats, the Trump administration rolled out inhumane immigration policies and promoted false narratives that promoted racism and discrimination.

Leftists argued that President Trump did not do nearly enough to address mass incarceration; negated the LGBTQ agenda and further weakening the ability of Americans to obtain adequate health care that put people's health and safety at risk.

Blah, blah, blah.

Jimmy Carter constantly harped on human rights as his mantra for the exclusion of all other issues, making him one of the worst presidents in history.

Donald Trump is not Carter. He will go down as one of the greatest leaders in our republic because he focused on the issues that define a great country.

The liberals bleated, "President Trump did not promote human rights abroad!" That wasn't his job, you wussy wimps. He was elected to make America *stronger,* not North Korea or Venezuela.

When it came to terrorism, ISIS, Al Qaeda, and dictatorship, Trump was the most effective President since Ronald Reagan.

Liberals hated him, too.

Criminal Legal System

We have the highest criminal incarceration rate in the world. 2.2 million people in prisons and jails. The female rate increased tremendously by 750% from 1980 to 2017.

You go, girls!

Racial disparities are obvious in the prison population. The imprisonment rate for black men is six times the rate for white men. It is even more disproportionate for younger black men.

Thank you, street gangs and drive-by shootings.

The death penalty is still allowed in 29 states but rarely executed. Only 20 people in seven states were put to death in 2019, mainly in the Southern and Midwestern states, led by Texas.

The bleeding heart pansies in California have a meaningless "death row" consisting of 730 condemned prisoners wasting taxpayer's money because they no longer engage in capital punishment.

Ridiculous.

Poor people take up way too much space in prison because they're too broke to afford bail. The rules badly need to be changed to fix that problem, especially for prisoners who have committed minor crimes.

Let's eliminate money bail, folks.

Children in the Criminal Justice System

An average day sees 50,000 children held in confinement!

This is patently unnecessary and absurd.

In addition, all 50 states continue to prosecute children in *adult* criminal courts. Yep, 32,000 children under 18 are admitted every year to adult jails.

Oregon and Washington D.C. are progressively trying to change that trend. So far, 22 states have followed their lead and now prohibit juvenile life sentences without parole.

But minorities and the poor are still getting the shaft. Believe me, prisons are not overflowing with *white* people!

If you're a person of color and you commit a crime, you are much more likely to spend years in prison than your Caucasian counterparts in 37 out of 50 states.

The solution for this imbalance begins and ends in the local communities where minorities are targeted for incarceration rather than counseling. So the homeless, mental health issues, and gangs pretty much doom blacks and Hispanics from staying out of jail.

In our largest cities, the mayor and city council are Democrats. Do we expect them to follow through on their phony rhetoric that they are the party of the underdog and less fortunate?

Hell no!

They don't care about the down and out except on election day. Democrats see minorities as votes, pure and simple. They are not going to spend civic money on people of color.

Democratic-run cities don't care if blacks kill blacks or Hispanics kill Hispanics as long as they are kept in their place.

This is one of America's dirty little secrets. Politicians don't want immigration reform, prison reform, or social reform because that will bring about change that could truly help the needy.

Instead, they play this game of charades in cahoots with the media pretending they are concerned about crime and black people. Yadda, yadda, yadda.

Reforms could take away their power and City Hall, which is dominated by black mayors and liberals, are not willing to give up.

Rather than address problems of poverty with services, support, and economic development, which could transform a city, these snakes in the grass deliberately ignore the solutions and decry the problems pretending they are sympathetic to their crime-infested communities.

Disgusting.

The mayors either add more police or push to defund the police, depending on which is more politically expedient now.

The consequences of this ongoing community mismanagement are *increased* incarcerations, naturally.

If you don't believe me, check out the history of the inner cities in Chicago, Baltimore, St. Louis, Minneapolis, Seattle, Detroit, and New York, for starters.

The status quo favors the liberals and day after day innocent people suffer.

It is a vicious cycle that needs a radical transformation beginning with replacing liberal and black mayors sooner than later to give our nation's cities a chance to flourish.

In 2019, police shot and killed almost 800 people. Of those killed, 20% were black, although blacks only made up 13% of the population. Racial disparities in non-fatal crimes were also rampant.

Poverty and Inequality

In September 2019, the Census Bureau released a study showing that income inequality in the U.S. had hit its highest level in five *decades!*

That translates to 40 million people now living in poverty with most of them making the minimum wage of $7.25 an hour.

Court-mandated fines and fees disproportionately impact poor citizens of color. When a financially strapped person cannot *afford* to pay these fines, they face arrest warrants, extended sentences, and, in many cases, incarceration.

These monies go to the funds of local jurisdictions gleefully accepting these free assets to continue their corrupt ways. Even a fine for jaywalking bolsters their money fund.

Reform needs to be targeted at these unethical cities that act as scavengers against their own citizens.

In summary, making our country great again begins and ends at the voting booths across America. We cannot expect a leopard to change its spots or a Democrat to give up his or her power.

A viper is a viper is a viper.

Donald Trump proclaimed, "Drain the Swamp!" Our great cities have fallen into disrepair, stained by deliberate policies to enslave people like modern-day plantation owners and saturated with corruption.

Until we get conservatives back in power, there will be racism, more incarceration, and inequality among those who have and those who have not.

This country was formed and flourished by Caucasian conservative and moderate men, not people of color, women, or liberals.

If that sounds harsh, it's not, it's factual. We began a downward social and political slide in the 1960s.

Our national leadership, beginning with LBJ and continuing with Jimmy Carter, the Bushes (closet Democrats), Bill Clinton, Barack Obama, and the current buffoon in the White House, has been disastrous to our economy, our social progress, our crime rate, and our international standing in world events.

The greatest presidents we have had, from Washington to Lincoln to Eisenhower to Kennedy to Nixon to Reagan to Trump, all had one asset in common.

None of them were flaming liberals.

They were patriots that put America first, protected their citizens, stood up to foreign enemies, and were revered by the world.

We need sweeping changes to regain leaders like that again.

Our country deserves that. More importantly, its success *depends* on it.

CHAPTER SEVENTEEN

THE RED MENACE

"**Communism is not love. Communism is a hammer we use to crush the enemy.**" Mao Tse-Tung

The late Party leader of Red China, formally known as Mao Zedong, was a bloodthirsty dictator responsible for killing 65 million of his citizens from 1935 until his death in 1976.

Of all the infamous world leaders in history, Mao was the most vicious and dangerous. He ruled his nation with an iron fist.

If you got in his way, you died.

He exiled his main rival, Chiang Kai-shek, to Taiwan permanently and forever. Kai-Shek is lucky to be alive.

"The Red Menace" was one of the greatest understatements in political history. Even with this evil man's death, China hasn't missed a beat in pursuing world dominance by any means possible.

The key to achieving that goal is the elimination of the United States of America. The leaders that have succeeded Mao are doing everything they can to take us down.

So, here is a three-word adage to always remember,

"Don't Trust China!"

They hate us.

They are constantly plotting against us.

They are relentless in conquering us.

They will use every means to eliminate us.

They will never be our allies.

"Don't Trust China!"

If you believe that the coronavirus was *accidentally* produced in a Chinese lab, you have the IQ of a kumquat.

There is no question the Chinese government commissioned its scientists to not only develop this killer disease and made certain it was transported by several Chinese airlines to our major cities.

This was as accidental as a firing squad.

Worse yet, it was financed and enabled by several influential Americans!

Of course, many of them vigorously denied any involvement in this deadly exercise and have avoided detection as a result.

All you do is research the American traitors that own major shares of stock in the vaccines to combat this killer virus.

You will see names like Bill Gates, Nancy Pelosi, Barack Obama and the headline hog, Dr. Fauci, all getting rich on the profits from their investments.

Not only has Covid-19 resulted in the deaths of thousands of innocent Americans, it brought down one of the greatest Presidents in our history and left us flailing with The Great Delusion and his goofy V.P.

Joe Biden sat on his butt in his basement during the entire campaign, only venturing out occasionally to accuse President Trump of mismanaging the virus and killing millions of innocent Americans.

That was his *singular* campaign message. He hustled back to his bunker to await further instructions from his Socialist handlers.

His ratings are now at 33% and still plummeting. Even the Democratic leadership is backing away from him.

Joe Biden has been a disaster in every sense of the word, much to the delight of the Chinese government, Biden's #1 ally in the world.

This isn't rocket science, folks. Even a first-grader can do the math on this one.

We have a President that is controlled by the Socialist/liberal agenda in the United States and the Chinese Communists internationally,

I could argue successfully that what China did to us was an Act of War. Killing millions of our citizens by placing a deadly virus in our atmosphere was far worse than the nerve gas the Germans used in World War II or Agent Orange our soldiers suffered in Vietnam.

"Don't Trust China!"

A top American virologist offered a chilling take on where we stand today with Covid-19.

"Reaching the end of this pandemic is impossible. We can only hope to get it down to *manageable* levels."

This is more than sobering, ladies and gentlemen. The idea that this virus will be with us forever, complete with masks, social distancing, and new mutations, is an American tragedy of the highest proportions.

The strong possibility that it was created and manipulated by our insidious enemy with the aid of an ultra-liberal political party and a corrupt media is unthinkable.

This sequence of events has not only taken thousands of lives, but it has also *ruined* millions of lives.

Lets not forget the other red menace from Russia, Vladimir Putin, who at this moment is trying to overtake the country of Ukraine with the barbaric treatment of the innocent citizens who refuse to adapt to his communist ways of living. **Don't Trust Russia"**

My prayer is that American voters will wake up and effect a change in the elections of 2022 and 2024 and sweep the Democrats out of power before they can do more damage to our way of life.

CHAPTER EIGHTEEN

THE CONSUMMATE CON MAN OF CALIFORNIA

"My fellow Californians, it's either me or the abyss." Gavin Newsom

With Gavin Newsom as your governor, it's both! Pick your poison, Golden Staters.

Either languish in the depths of his deceitful administration or somehow tolerate his insufferable narcissism as he uses California as a steppingstone to the White House.

This man has no shame.

The last group of people he looks out for are his constituents. It's all about himself. He had a good teacher.

His aunt is Nancy Pelosi.

The apple doesn't fall from the tree.

His most enthusiastic supporters are public-employee unions, which greatly rake in millions of dollars from the state's cash cow funds.

These leeches collect a billion dollars every year in *forced* membership fees thanks to his governing generosity which takes advantage of the average California voter.

What does the crafty and calculating con man do with all those kickbacks?

Pay handsomely to all the well-heeled lobbyists and their consultants who gleefully do their bidding. The man is a political hustler.

If you enjoy being nauseous, check out the numbers. Governor Con Man's 2021 budget spent $455 BILLION in state and federal funds!

Half of those billions were spent on federal pass-through dollars for local assistance, which was tied to various stimulus packages to keep dozens of his state's corrupt cities in force instead of folding due to bankruptcy.

Newsom needs his cities to keep his empire alive.

If you're wondering that this money was carefully laundered for a noble purpose like Covid-19, forget it. He was manipulating funding long *before* we had a pandemic.

Of course, these financial machinations don't solve California's massive debt problems, it has an opposite effect, saddling the state with years of financial spending and leaving it constantly on the edge of bankruptcy.

Newsom's mantra "Other People's Money" translates to "Future People's Problems!"

By the time California will have to pay the piper, he plans to be running the country into the ground from the Oval Office.

Or relaxing on a beach resort somewhere enjoying his net worth of $20 million which is almost certain to increase significantly with each passing year.

The real Gavin Newsom: **Anatomy of a con man.**

Charming

At the core of an effective, confident man is likability. Newsom convinces people he is a good guy. His sparkling personality hides a devious Socialistic agenda.

Like Barack Obama and Bill Clinton, he sells himself as the neighbor you would enjoy having a beer with at a backyard barbecue.

Don't be fooled here.

The true essence of these men is saturated with a need for power and money. They are as ruthless in their ambition to rule the innocents of the world.

Shameless

Having a conscience and caring about right from wrong is a noble quality. Unfortunately,

most politicians lack this gene. They don't function in an ethical universe, but one laden with lobbyists, special interest groups, unions, backroom deals, and financial kickbacks.

Their advisors and aides are constantly telling them to take advantage of their opportunities. These "yes men and women" have no conscience, either.

Most politicians only care about two things: getting re-elected and padding their income.

Elitist

Governor Con Man has two sets of rules, one for his minions and one for himself. Here is a tweet from the Governor's office to the citizens of California,

"Going out to eat with members of your household this weekend? Don't forget to keep your mask on in between bites. Do your part to keep those around you healthy."

But apparently, Governor Con Man didn't read his own memo.

On November 18, 2020, Newsom and his dinner guests were shown having a grand old time at a birthday party in Napa, California.

Without masks or social distancing.

OOPS!

Do as I say, don't do as I do, huh Guv?

Condescending

Gavin Newsom believes himself to be the smartest person in the room. He looks down on people. His policies constantly reflect he is an intellectual giant among his fellow citizens in California.

If he decides to raise outrageous gasoline taxes, he does it. End of story. There is no debate here. He says it, you believe it and that is the law.

His arrogance is unparalleled compared to the chief executive officer of his state. This is the main reason residents are fleeing California to other states.

Two words.

Governor Newsom.

The Insufferable Big Head.

Californians not only dislike his ultra-liberal policies, but they also don't like him *personally* as evidenced by a recall petition they put to a vote in 2020.

He survived the recall which only increased his delusion that he was all that and a bag of chips.

Politically astute.

Newsom is a sharp cookie. He is a man among boys when it comes to political savvy. He knows how to turn on the charm and when to back off.

Newsom also knows what battles to fight and which ones to ignore. He has an innate genius about knowing when to attack and when to retreat.

The governor is as sharp as a tack. It would not surprise me if he won the Presidency someday. But it would be disastrous for our country.

Alpha Dog Democrat

Gavin Newsom is the political king of California. Democrats dominate the state, and he dominates the Democrats. He is securely protected and revered in his political nest. No one can touch him.

He has the right to be elitist and arrogant. He always gets his way and that is going to be the case as governor.

California will keep losing residents, but Newsom doesn't care. Every time someone moves to another state, he becomes more powerful.

And he knows it.

CHAPTER NINETEEN

ME RUN FOR GOVERNOR... WHY NOT?

"Be hungry for success, hungry to make your mark, hungry to be seen and to be heard and to have an effect. And as you move up and become successful, make sure also to be hungry for helping others." Arnold Schwarzenegger

What if I considered running for governor in the state of California?

Why?

Because I have a passion to help others. I do not believe the current office holder has that same motivation. He is a politician, not a man of the people.

Gavin Newsom is an elitist. He has two sets of rules, one for him and one for everyone else.

He makes all these rules for his citizens like social distancing, wearing masks, and avoiding close encounters with friends and family.

Then, he goes out and ignores those rules.

It is not a responsible public servant. That is a hypocrite.

The people of California deserve better. Much better!

If I were to run against him, I would have to overcome several obstacles.

Financing

You need millions to become the governor of this state. I lack that ability, and worse yet, I am not willing to accept bribes, payoffs, and kickbacks from unsavory lobbyists and unions.

Gavin Newsom is a master of raising money and taking care of the individuals and groups that support him.

I won't do that. I would have to build my campaign on common people with good hearts donating small amounts, so I am not ripping them off or being bought by unethical characters.

Lack of name recognition

No one in power has ever heard of Richard Lira. I am a mystery to them. I would have to spend 2-3 years developing familiarity with voters.

A daunting challenge.

It can be done.

Few voters had ever heard of an obscure peanut farmer named Jimmy Carter when he ran for the governor of Georgia, although he served for a brief time as a state senator in the legislature.

So, I would have to be elected to something beyond dog catcher to build my qualifications along with my name.

Maybe I could run for state assembly or county supervisor first.

Speaking ability

I'm a talker and a very persuasive one at that. I can impress audiences with my verbal charm.

Author

Most candidates for higher office have written a popular book that endeared them to voters.

John F. Kennedy wrote *"Profiles in Courage"* which won a Pulitzer Prize.

It detailed heroic individuals that captured America's attention even though there is strong evidence that his speechwriter, Theodore Sorenson, wrote most of the book.

Either way, I need a book.

Campaign issues

I will need to tell the voters of California what I stand for so they can support my political agenda. At this point in time, here are the main planks in my platform,

Trim and balance our bloated budget
Immigration Fairness
Eliminate high taxes on consumer use
Parents should decide on mask mandates for kids, not the schools or unions
Lift all weapons bans in the state. We have
The right to defend ourselves
Open all restaurants and outdoor venues
Give the option of wearing a mask to the people of California

End the politics of Covid-19
Keep the crooks away from power
Repudiate liberal politics
Slash bureaucratic regulations
Returning California to a Red state
Available to my voters
Cut off special interest parasites
Bring back the Presence of God
Almighty
Enable Californians to smile more
Make California Great Again

As I mentioned earlier, the challenges facing me make it darn near impossible for my dream here to become a reality. But that's what dreams are for, right?

If you're going to live for something worth dying for then dream *big!*

I see the potential for my state to flourish under my administration. I just need financial resources, good campaign people around me, a strong political agenda, and a few breaks along the way.

Larry Elder failed in his attempt to recall Newsom. I liked Larry, he was a good guy and a wonderful Christian.

But to beat Newsom you need to be more charismatic and stand out among the voters.

It can be done. There is no question in my mind about that.

I need to passionately believe I am the one to do it. I'm not there yet.

If I ever do make that campaign leap, you will be the first to know.

If this is God's will for me, I will obey Him.

"You have to dream before your dreams can come true. Hold fast to dreams, for if dreams die, life is a broken-winged bird that cannot fly. To accomplish great things, we must not only act but also dream; not only plan but also believe." P.J. Abdul Kalam

CHAPTER TWENTY

MAKING AMERICA GREAT AGAIN

"**What has made America great has been the opportunities given to everyone in this country. Since our founding, individuals and families have come to America to seek freedom, opportunity, and the choice for a better life.**" Cathy McMorris

There was a father who was reading his evening newspaper and being constantly interrupted by his four-year-old son.

Finally, to distract the child so he could finish his reading, he challenged the boy, "I want you to solve a puzzle!"

The young lad looked quizzically at his father and asked, "What puzzle?"

The father saw a map of the United States and took his scissors and cut out each state and put them on the floor. "This is America, I want you to assemble all of these states and show me what America looks like!"

The boy exclaimed, "I can do that!"

The father chuckled and went back to his paper, confident that the little guy would take hours trying to solve the puzzle.

In less than five minutes, the map of the United States was perfectly organized to the consternation of the parent.

"Son, how did you do that, son?" He asked with a stunned look on his face.

"It was easy, dad. On the other side of the puzzle was a picture of a man and I put that together and flipped it over and America was right!"

This metaphor reveals a powerful truth: if all men were put together properly, our country would take shape!

So, what are the qualities American citizens need to possess to make our nation great again?

Here they are in their red, white, and blue glory!

A Devotion to America

Every citizen from Maine to Mississippi and from Washington to West Virginia needs to be sold out to our nation's values and way of life.

Party affiliation, ideologies, and race must all take a back seat to the land we love. America FIRST, end of the story. We need passionate citizens willing to die for their belief in our republic, just like the early colonists.

We are in a war today as big as the one that we fought against the British in 1775. It is an internal battle *within* our country, not with an enemy abroad.

Liberals, socialists, domestic terrorists, misguided racists like Black Lives Matter, Antifa, far-left extremists, the toxic media, the haters of the Constitution, abortionists, and the corrupt politicians in Washington constantly undermining our freedoms, need to be **vanquished** to save our nation from ruin.

We need a patriotic remnant of our great country to stand up and fight with every inch of their being to Make America Great Again. This is not just a clever phrase promoted by Ronald Reagan and Donald Trump, it is a battle cry that needs to be embedded in the souls of true Americans and executed powerfully over the next fifty years and beyond.

Would you die for your country?

I would. Damn right, I would!

A Love of Liberty

Historically, millions of fighting men and women went to battle to keep our country free in several wars. They shed their blood to preserve the values set forth by our Founding Fathers.

Amendments to our Constitution detail those freedoms. They are the lifeblood of our nation's breathing apparatus. They are the life support for every move America makes in our way of life.

Freedom differentiates us from most nations in the world. We not only need to appreciate it, we need to *preserve* it! The only way that can happen is for individual Americans to commit themselves to the liberty our statesmen and soldiers cherish so highly.

We can never be casual about this, or we will let it slip away and our country will disappear along with it.

That must never happen.

Tolerance

I'm not asking you to blindly accept evil here. Tolerance is an acceptance and respect for diversity, people, or situations that differ from yours.

It is a positive celebration of the various faces and views of America. We need to honor all beliefs, cultures, religions, and colors of our fellow citizens.

It is respecting the character of good people that come from backgrounds and lifestyles unlike ours. Real freedom is based upon our ability to accept humanity, not condemn it.

That does not mean we embrace hurtful behaviors or ideologies. It does mean that we adhere to the U.S. Constitution's mandate that **"all free men be equally created to have the same treatment under the law, and the same ability to question and abolish the government creating those laws. "**

That includes Caucasians, minorities, men, women, straight, gay, transgender, young people, seniors, and all those that live in America, if they are not breaking our laws or trying to destroy it.

We are not better than anyone else and no one else is better than us. We are all *equal* under the law. **Just getting along and supporting each other in this country would be a huge step forward in making our nation greater, for starters.**

Enough fighting already!

It needs to begin in the U.S. Congress so our political leaders can learn to work together in a bi-partisan way to improve the quality of life for its citizens.

My dream is that it permeates the heart and soul of every American citizen.

I'm so tired of all the fighting, aren't you?

A profound reverence for our service heroes

I am talking about the courageous men and women who serve in the military, law enforcement, firefighters, doctors, nurses, coaches, teachers, tutors, mentors, pastors, priests, nuns, rabbis, community leaders, and volunteers, for starters.

These individuals not only protect the backbone of America, but they are also the backbone of America!

It angers me when I see any of these groups disrespected. That's not American, that's hating.

If we are to be great again, we need to cherish and honor these remarkable individuals and groups.

Thousands have sacrificed their time, energy, income, and even their lives to preserve our freedom. They are truly heroes and should be *honored* as such.

National Pride

America: Love it or LEAVE it!

I stand by that statement. If you don't like it here, get the hell out!

We are the greatest nation on earth. We need to be proud of that. We need to embrace it.

I feel incredibly blessed to have grown up in the United States of America. The rest of the world envies us and they should.

Our laws were brilliantly crafted by the Founding Fathers, our national landmarks are epic, our symbols of freedom are powerful, our democracy and love for capitalism have made us the American Dream and our people are the most colorful, friendliest, and smartest in the world.

We have charming towns, fabulous cities, and a unique set of states. We evolve positively every day and just keep getting better.

We have a lot to be proud of in America. We need to express that pride wherever we are in or out of our wonderful nation.

If you don't like it, don't let the door hit your ass on the way to the airport!

A Constitutional Commitment

Read and absorb the documents that shaped our Republic, the Declaration of Independence, the Bill of Rights, and the Constitution. The brilliant definitions formed by political intellectuals gave America its breadth and life.

We are not a dictatorship, nor will we ever be. Our legal foundations will always prevent that. The equanimity of our three branches of government, the Executive, the Legislative, and the Supreme Court, all hold each in check.

We have a perfect system of government. Even the toxic Democrats and nutcase liberals can't mess it up even though they are trying to.

Without our well-balanced Constitution, we would be susceptible to dictatorship, communism, or mired in mediocrity.

Our system of laws is the finest on earth. We need to appreciate the power it affords us as a nation.

We are truly blessed.

Reliance on a Sovereign God

The final aspect of the American profile is the most vital. Recite the pledge of allegiance and listen carefully to your words,

"One nation, under God…"

Amen and amen.

"In God we trust" is also a staple of our republic. It is no coincidence that we have flourished as a nation for over two hundred years.

Even though there is no direct reference to God or Jesus in the Founding Fathers' documents, the American Constitution itself was founded upon *Biblical* standards.

We need to always honor Him as an individual and as a nation, for He is the sustenance of all that is holy and righteous in the world.

Most of our Constitutional writers and crafters were Christians or Deists. They did not believe in a "hands-on God" minutely directing everything we do as a country, but as a background figure of support to guarantee ethical and legal support to keep America grounded in righteousness.

The little boy who put together the figure of the man and then flipped the puzzle over to reveal the map of the United States was spot on. If all American citizens possessed the attributes of what I have just listed, our country would take shape in awesome ways.

CHAPTER TWENTY-ONE

WHY I LOVE AMERICA

I am so grateful that I was born and raised in the United States of America! What a great country.

Let's begin with the most incredible document any nation can possess.

The Constitution.

The Founding Fathers drafted brilliantly when they laid the foundation for our laws detailing our freedoms.

No other country comes close in its explanation of how a people should be governed!

Here are some powerful excerpts outlining our cherished liberty under the blessing of God.

"We, the People of the United States, in order to form a more perfect Union, establish Justice, insure domestic Tranquility, provide for the common defence, promote the general Welfare, and secure the Blessings of Liberty to ourselves and our Posterity, do

ordain and establish this Constitution for the United States of America."

It's the guiding force behind the most enduring democratic system of government ever; it helped create the environment that produced the greatest economic engine in history; it's been used as a model for better government around the world.

The great minds of patriotic Americans wholeheartedly endorse this document. This is what makes our Republic great.

"The Constitution is the guide which I will never abandon." **George Washington**

"The happy Union of these States is a wonder; their Constitution a miracle; their example the hope of Liberty throughout the world." **James Madison**

"The glory of justice and the majesty of law are created not just by the Constitution - nor by the courts - nor by the officers of the law - nor by the lawyers - but by the men and women who constitute our society - who are the protectors of the law as they are themselves protected by the law." **Robert F. Kennedy**

"The U.S. Constitution doesn't guarantee happiness, only the pursuit of it. You have to catch up with it yourself." **Benjamin Franklin**

"We still have the oldest written constitution still in force in the world, and it starts out with three words: 'We, the people.'" **Ruth Bader Ginsburg**

I love the Declaration of Independence expressing our separation from British rule and establishing our independent nation. In Congress, July 4, 1776

Thomas Jefferson

The unanimous Declaration of the thirteen United States of America,

When, during the course of human events, it becomes necessary for one people to *dissolve* the political bands which have connected them with another, and to assume among the powers of the earth, the separate and equal station to which the Laws of Nature and of Nature's God entitle them, a decent respect to the opinions of mankind requires that they should declare the causes which impel them to the separation.

We hold these truths to be self-evident, that all men are created equal, that they are endowed by their Creator with certain unalienable Rights, that among these are Life, Liberty, and the pursuit of Happiness.

To secure these rights, governments are instituted among men, deriving their just powers from the consent of the governed,

That whenever any Form of Government becomes destructive to these ends, it is the Right of the People to alter or to abolish it, and to institute new Government, laying its foundation on such principles and organizing its powers in such form, as to them shall seem most likely to affect their Safety and Happiness. Prudence. Indeed,

The **United States Bill of Rights** comprises the first ten amendments to the United States Constitution.

The Bill of Rights amendment adds to the Constitution specific guarantees of personal freedoms and rights, clear limitations on the government's power in judicial and other proceedings, and explicit declarations that all powers not specifically granted to the federal government by the Constitution are reserved to the states or the people.

I love America because we are a historical tradition. Everywhere I look, I see majestic greatness from Lady Liberty in New York's harbor and the promise of the American Dream to the chiseled countenances of our four remarkable presidents at Rushmore to the red, white, and blue of our patriotic flag.

I love the sight of the soaring bald eagle symbolizing the unlimited opportunity America offers, and the Lincoln Memorial reminds us that all men are created equal.

I love the stateliest residence in the world, the center of power that leaves all the nations in awe.

The White House.

When you walk from there to the U.S. Capitol and end up on the Supreme Court, you capture the perfect balance of power that keeps the Executive, the Legislative, and the Judicial in check, preserving leadership, fairness, and justice within boundaries.

I love our natural beauty, from the awe-inspiring Grand Canyon to the meandering Mississippi to the breathtaking Manhattan skyline to the unforgettable sunsets of the Pacific Ocean.

I love our great cities, the lakefront of Chicago, the jazz of New Orleans, the Golden Gate of San Francisco, the revolutionary reminders of Boston and Philadelphia, and the hustle and bustle of New York City.

I love the feelings and sensations of America, the smell of sage and yucca in the high desert of California, the feeling of the ocean breeze as it permeates my hair, a rhythmic rainfall while I am reading a book over a cup of hot tea, the sun peeking through the mountains in the east, waking me up to begin a new and exciting day, the falling snow on Christmas Eve, the smell of smoke in the air in the fall and, the first budding blooms in New England and Atlanta signaling the end of winter.

I love the American holidays because they represent much more than a day off, they stand for the greatness of men and women that fought for them to exist in the first place.

Martin Luther King Day eloquently states, "I have a dream that my four little children will one day live in a nation where they will not be judged by the color of their skin but by the content of their character."

Memorial Day weekend honors those who lost their lives in battle defending our nation.

Labor Day is a tribute to the working men and women who toil faithfully to keep our country going.

Veteran's Day is giving respect to all who served in the military. Thanksgiving is a feast of gratitude where we thank the Almighty for our blessings, beginning with our freedom.

The Fabulous 4th of July, America's birthday, is an explosion of fireworks, patriotic songs, and pride that we live in the greatest nation on earth!

I love the first Tuesday in November, Election Day, a powerful evening that guarantees the transfer of power in America that is decided by the vote of the people and not the villainous machinations of a tyrant.

I love the heroes who fought for America immortalized by Arlington Cemetery, The Tomb of the Unknown Soldier, The

Pearl Harbor Memorial, The Vietnam Wall, The 9/11 Memorial, Lexington Green, and Gettysburg.

I love the creativity and entertainment value of American arts, Gladys Knight, Rock n' Roll, Motown, Johnny Cash, Ray Charles, the genres of pop, jazz, blues, and country, that have given me thousands of hours of listening pleasure.

Only in America would you be amazed by the athletic exploits of Kobe Bryant, Sandy Koufax, USC football, UCLA basketball, the LA Rams, the LA Dodgers, and the Showtime Lakers!

I love the American people from all walks of life, a melting pot of diversity from East LA to farmer's fields to Surf City to Texas ranchers and the Alaskan pipeline.

Everyday Americans that grow up serving our society as police officers, firefighters, EMTs, doctors, nurses, and soldiers put their lives on the line to protect us from terrorists, domestic and foreign.

The honor and unselfishness of Americans bring tears to my eyes when I think of their heroism and sacrifice to protect us and preserve our way of life.

Yes, I love America for a thousand reasons, and I am proud to live here, raise my children here and die here.

God bless the United States, always and forever.

CHAPTER TWENTY-TWO

COLIN KAEPERNICK, GEORGE FLOYD, AND BLACK LIVES MATTER

"You know what I say about all this garbage, about racism being everywhere? It's a cynical political power play by Democrats that needs to end quickly before we get to a race war they arc hell-bent on starting. I'm really sick of watching America being ripped in half over racism by so-called progressive Democrats and their shameless flacks and lackeys in the media." Michael Reagan

I am not a racist. I believe in the truism that all men are created equally. I am dead set against politicians and celebrities who use *racism* as a weapon and a rationalization to unethically further their agenda.

The race card is the most popular brand of the far left and it is as pathetic as it is transparent. For starters, Bill and Hillary Clinton, Barack Obama, and most of the leading liberals have done virtually nothing for black people.

They are all talk and no action.

It's been that way for generations.

The Ku Klux Klan was invented on three different occasions, not by Republicans but by Democrats. In fact, it was the first Republican President, Abraham Lincoln, that created The Emancipation Proclamation, effectively ending slavery.

In the 1960 presidential race, it was Richard Nixon who was close friends with Martin Luther King, not John F. Kennedy.

The only reason Kennedy used his influence to free Dr. King from jail was that it would gain him thousands of black voters. Bobby Kennedy was furious when he found out that his brother had helped King.

As it turned out, that move was a major reason JFK became President. That's the same reason why Democrats pretend they are pro-black today, not out of principle, but for more political power.

During the Clinton and Obama administrations, there was very little legislation that improved the quality of black life. In contrast, the numbers helping blacks and their families, unemployment, living wages, and tax benefits under Donald Trump were spectacular.

No president has ever seen such progress since Lincoln.

Yes, President Trump is a Republican.

Democrats are insidious hypocrites when it comes to helping minorities. Only if it benefits their political agenda will they lift a finger in support.

A revealing example of this is the George Floyd incident. I am sad that he died during his arrest, but the real reason he did is still murky. He was on major drugs at the time, and they could have cost his life as much and not the police.

Floyd was a thug, a convicted felon. But by the time the Democrats lionized him, he was right up there with Martin Luther King and Rosa Parks.

I am surprised there isn't a national holiday named after him.

The way the liberals have been praising him for no real reason shows their lack of common sense and character. This is not an American hero, and neither was Rodney King, Al Sharpton, Jesse Jackson, or any of the other race-baiters that cleverly stoked the fires of discontent in America.

Colin Kaepernick and his mission to discredit the national anthem by tying it to police brutality against blacks is a joke. Kaepernick has always been a confused young man in search of attention. He wanted to be famous, and he found his five minutes of fame, manipulating black people to believe that the police were killing all their kin. In truth, white cops kill white criminals in more cases than blacks. But another statistic is more telling prisons and jails are filled with more blacks than whites.

Is the prison system racist, too?

Please explain to me how the National Anthem is to blame for policemen doing their job? Only a confused ex-quarterback and an angry minority population can answer that question.

Then you have thousands of athletes jumping on the Kaepernick bandwagon as though they were the savviest of politicians. Lebron James, who never went to college, is now the sage of society as he uses his ability to dunk a basketball as credibility on the racial agenda.

Ridiculous.

Just when we thought that racism was out of hand along came Black Lives Matter to throw gasoline on the black and white debate.

This group has two brains, one is lost, and the other is out looking for it.

Of course, black lives matter, I have no problem with that premise because ALL lives matter. Hispanic lives matter, Asian lives matter, Native American lives matter, Caucasian lives matter…duh!

There is nothing uniquely special about black life that forces us to believe it matters more than any other race.

Try to tell that to the #1 racist in America, Barack Obama, who injected himself into the racial discussion and did all he could to give credibility to BLM, giving them a national platform with a presidential blessing.

It is a fact in history that Obama will go down as the most racially divisive President in history. This is not my opinion, this is his factual legacy, folks.

As a result, under the guise of "racial justice," we have seen cities like Portland, Seattle, Charlottesville, Minneapolis, Chicago, Los Angeles, and Kenosha, for starters, all devastated by the glee of the liberal Democrats who used this violence and thuggery as a weapon against law-abiding officials.

Obama, Biden, Kamala Harris, Bernie Sanders, and other hate-mongers encouraged the criminal activity and looting in these towns and constantly exclaimed, "Defund the police!" one of the most moronic ideas in American history.

Racism is subjective. If a white or black citizen believes something is racist, then it is. There are no grounds for facts because you can't debate opinions no matter how non-sensical they are.

But erecting a hero statue of a criminal, George Floyd, giving credence to a blatantly racist President, destroying our traditional monuments, believing that only black lives matter, and kneeling out of protest towards our national anthem is more than misguided, it is a targeted plot to destroy America.

See-through the lies, my fellow citizens. Don't let the tactics of hate and racial manipulation fool you. Stand firm against these people.

Our nation's freedom depends on it.

CHAPTER TWENTY-THREE

RATING THE PRESIDENT'S GOOD AND BAD

"In many cases, voters on election day don't vote for a President, they vote *against* the candidate they don't want for a President or the lesser of two evils. Examples include Goldwater in '64, McGovern in '72, Jimmy Carter in '80, Dukakis in '88, Hillary in 2016, and Trump in 2020."

Let's be candid here.

In the past 60+ years, we have had a myriad of presidential elections on the first Tuesday in November and the outcome of many of them stirred strong emotions because of the candidates involved.

I am going to list my five least favorite Presidents and my four favorites.

When someone you loathe becomes President, you are stuck with that chief executive for 4-8 years and it is a miserable existence.

Here are my takes on the least qualified Presidents since 1964, followed by my personal favorites.

#5 Bill Clinton. Truthfully, "Slick Willie" had a pretty good presidency, but he brought a ton of immoral baggage with him to the White House, including his unethical wife, Hillary.

He also brought a sex scandal with him, too.

This led to his impeachment, which almost cost him the office. When you think of Bill Clinton today, you don't recall his economic programs or his foreign success with terrorism.

No.

You can automatically link him to Monica Lewinsky. She is his legacy, and it will follow him to his grave.

Like Richard Nixon, William Jefferson Clinton made an indelible imprint on history for the wrong reasons.

#4 Father and son Bush. Our country could have been so much better had neither of these buffoons been elected to the highest office in the land.

The dad dramatically promised at his nominating convention, "Read my lips, NO NEW TAXES." which turned out to be a lie.

His four years in office were so unremarkable that only defeating Iraq in the Gulf War prevented him from being invisible.

His son, George W., had an inept domestic policy compared to most Presidents, so he diverted the attention of his failed agenda there to take down Saddam Hussein, who somehow was blamed for 9/11, when it was obvious that ¾ of the plane terrorists were from Saudi Arabia, one of our oil allies!

The two charlatans were Democrat wolves dressed in Republican sheep suits.

George W. was not the smartest leader to occupy the Oval Office, but he sparkled as a host of his famous barbecues on his Texas ranch.

Probably because he doesn't have to pronounce words with more than one syllable to his guests.

#3 Jimmy Carter. The knock-on Carter was that he could describe the intricacies of a nuclear submarine, he just couldn't *steer* it!

He couldn't steer our country, either.

Carter was constantly going on television to try to explain away his gaffes to no avail. America went from one crisis to another under its watch: inflation, gas shortages, the Iran hostage crisis, and an impotent foreign policy.

Finally, Jimmy went on television and announced that the American people had a "crisis of confidence." We needed to be more optimistic, he chortled.

His analysis was misplaced. We had not lost confidence in America but in HIM!

He was awarded for his awful performance as President in 1980 by getting soundly spanked by Ronald Reagan and returned to his peanut farm in Plains, Georgia, where he belonged.

#2 Barack Obama. How an obscure Senator from Illinois was elected President of the United States, only a drunken Democrat voter could explain!

He has been out of his league from Day One. He began by apologizing to the world that America had a history of imperialism and we had been very insensitive to foreign countries that deserved better.

He began donning Muslim outfits and tried to pass himself off as an Islamic devotee. He collaborated with the organizers of "Black Lives Matter" further alienating the rest of the country that was non-black.

Obama did his best to emulate the segregationist George Wallace. His legacy will go down as the most divisive racist in presidential history. When scores of white Dallas police officers were cut down by black gunmen over a two-week period, Obama stood by and said nothing.

The most remarkable thing Obama did was put together a campaign coalition of 47% which included a potpourri of niche voters, women, young people, blacks, Hispanics, gays, welfare recipients and food stampers.

Running against very fallible candidates Mitt Romney and John McCain in successive elections didn't hurt his chances, either.

We were stuck with this do-nothing "community organizer" with the silver tongue for eight years. It was a waste of America's time.

#1 Joe Biden. A by-product of Obama's legacy was that he introduced the Delusional Delaware Dunderhead to the presidential stage as his Veep.

Had he not done so, we wouldn't be suffering from "Bidenitis disease" today. His favorable polls have him at 33%, guaranteed to drop even more with each passing day.

Simply put, Joe Biden has no clue what he is doing.

We would have been better off with Eeyore in the White House. The only good thing about Biden's presidency is that he is blocking Kamala Harris from leading our nation.

Biden not only has difficulty passing legislation, but he also has trouble finishing sentences. Even worse, he doesn't realize he is brain-challenged.

He believes he is the true leader we have all been looking for, man!

Not even close.

Somewhere, the Founding Fathers are cringing in their graves, fearful that we won't survive this travesty of an administration.

The scary part is that many of the Democrat leaders are feeling the same thing.

Now, I submit to you my four favorite presidents of my life and my reasons for my choices.

#4 Richard Nixon. Take away Watergate and he is arguably the most accomplished President in American history.

Nixon ended the involuntary draft. He ended the Vietnam conflict. He established the Environmental Protection Agency (EPA), opened relationships with our two biggest enemies, Russia and China.

He was President during the first moon landing, he appointed four Supreme Court Justices to move the Court to the political right and he oversaw 100 million dollars to begin the war on cancer.

Nixon signed Title IX in 1972, opening the doors for women in collegiate sports. He oversaw the peaceful desegregation of southern schools. He also lowered the voting age from twenty-one to eighteen, giving young people a chance to vote.

He was the first President to give Native Americans the right to tribal self-determination and return their sacred lands to them.

He negotiated a truce in the SALT agreement with the Soviet Union bringing détente to the Cold War.

Nixon signed the ABM Treaty with Russia curtailing the threat of nuclear weapons between the two superpowers.

He established a new relationship with the Middle East, eliminating Soviet dominance in the region.

He initiated Project Independence, allowing the U.S. to end reliance on foreign oil by 1980. He saved Israel from Arab dominance by backing them in the 1973 Yom Kipper War.

Golda Meir stated, "Nixon saved our country."

I can see why the Democrats and liberals hated him. I loved him.

#3 Dwight Eisenhower. One of the greatest American patriots in our nation's history. He commanded the Allied Forces in World War II and oversaw the D-Day invasion that broke the back of the Nazis.

Eisenhower established NATO. He created the interstate highway system that revolutionized our highways and roads.

In 1957, he enacted the first significant civil rights legislation since 1975 and sent federal troops to Little Rock to implement it.

In 1960, he enacted the Civil Rights Act that established a federal inspection of local voter registration polls with penalties for anyone who obstructed someone's attempt to register to vote.

He founded NASA.

He presided over one of the most robust economies in American history. He helped Alaska and Hawaii achieve statehood.

He ended the Korean War by threatening China with nuclear weapons. He used the same threat on the Soviet Union to introduce the Cold War instead of nuclear annihilation.

He served as the President of Columbia University, a prestigious Ivy League school in New York City.

He won peace and presided over the amazing prosperity our nation has ever experienced, evidenced by balancing the national budget three times.

I have nothing but admiration for him.

#2 Donald Trump. The Democrats did everything they could to get him out of power because much of his legislation butted heads with their liberal and socialist agendas.

Trump introduced the Tax Cuts and Jobs Act, placing more money back into the pockets of Americans. This also puts our nation in a stronger position to fight the coronavirus when it hits us.

He established a secure border with Mexico and began rebuilding the wall when he lost his bid for re-election.

Our trade deals with foreign countries, even China, were both powerful and positive. Trump was a tough negotiator and made the United States a force to be reckoned with in the international trade community.

He deleted dozens of unnecessary regulatory barriers that Democrats had used to not only clog up the system but to use them as weapons in their partisan war with Republicans.

President Trump sent three new justices to the Supreme Court, giving conservatives a majority of 6-3 and the chance to reverse liberal travesties such as Roe v. Wade.

He built the most prosperous economy that America had seen in years, 7 million new jobs, middle-class family income increase more than $6,000, triple that of Obama's efforts, the unemployment rate reached a record LOW of 3.5%, the best in the past 50 years. More Americans were working than ever before, 160 million!

Incomes rose in every single metro area for the first time in three decades.

Unemployment rates for minorities, blacks, Hispanics, and Asians reached record lows.

The bottom 50% of American households saw a 40% INCREASE in net worth.

Blue-collar and low-income workers saw a 16% pay increase. Trump was truly a financially effective President!

He created more than 1.2 million manufacturing and construction jobs.

The DOW closed above 20,000 for the first time in 2017 and topped 30,000 in 2020.

Trump gave the typical family of four a $2,000 tax cut and doubled the child tax credit. He also virtually eliminated the estate tax.

Democrats had the business tax rate at 35%. Trump slashed it down to 21% and allowed small businesses to deduct 20% of their business income!

We need to get him back into the Oval Office!

#1 Ronald Reagan. This President first coined the term "Make America Great Again" and he did!

He made us feel better with his positive approach to politics. The dark shadows of the inept Jimmy Carter were obliterated in the sunshine of glowing optimism!

Reagan literally destroyed the Soviet Union with his Strategic Defense Initiative (SDI), which forced the Russian superpower to match it and shattered their economy.

As a result, the Soviet Union collapsed in 1991. Back in our country, Reaganomics allowed us to financially flourish.

In 1989, President Reagan chastised the Russian Premier Gorbachev to "Tear down that (Berlin) wall!" In November of that year, the wall came down for the first time since 1961.

It was a CELEBRATION of freedom-loving people everywhere!

His Reagan Doctrine mightily contributed to the demise of the Soviets. It allowed us to spend less than one billion a year while forcing the Russians to spend eight times that much to keep up with us.

It also caused the Soviets to pull out of Afghanistan, affected a democratic election in Nicaragua and removed 40,000 Cuban troops from Angola.

As Margaret Thatcher opined, "Ronald Reagan won the Cold War, not only without firing a shot but also by inviting enemies out of their fortress and turning them into friends."

He was truly a great President and my all-time favorite!

CHAPTER TWENTY-FOUR

WHAT IS A PATRIOT?

"**G**ive me liberty or give me death!" Patrick Henry

A person who vigorously supports their country and is prepared to defend it against enemies or detractors.

A true American patriot always ties his passion to freedom. He also links liberty to righteousness from God. Patriots have character.

They believe God is blessing their nation and they honor both His Sovereignty and their beloved homeland.

That is why they are willing to die for their country, as Patrick Henry stated.

Patriots vs. Loyalists

During the Revolutionary War, some of the Founding Fathers were patriots and some were loyalists. The fundamental *difference?*

A patriot was committed to the new colonies. A loyalist was still tied to the British government of King George III.

An example of this was Alexander Hamilton.

Over the 246 years since our nation was founded, we have had thousands of notable patriots that have been an honor to our country in all fields of renown.

It's funny that I am such a patriot. I even attended Theodore Roosevelt High School in Los Angeles.

Coincidence?

I think not!

I am a purebred and born American son who will defend my country to the death!

I love my fellow patriots. Here are some of the most remarkable ones,

George Washington

We begin with "The Father of our Country." There was no greater patriot than Washington. He led our emerging nation in the war effort, headed up the Founding Fathers, and was our first President.

Abraham Lincoln

A remarkable leader and President who abolished slavery and led us out of the Civil War. His quote here encompasses his patriotic passion for his nation,

"I would save the Union. I would save it the shortest way under the Constitution. ... If I could save the Union without freeing any slave I would do it, and if I could save it by

freeing all the slaves I would do it; and if I could save it by freeing some and leaving others alone, I would also do that."

Harriet Tubman

She escaped slavery as a young woman and went on to establish and maintain The Underground Railroad, a complex of tunnels and caves that allowed over 300 slaves to escape their captivity. She served bravely as a nurse and a spy for the Union military in the Civil War.

She risked her life to participate in a raid on a plantation in South Carolina that freed over 700 more slaves. Following the Civil War, she opened a home for aged and elderly African Americans.

Later in her life, she opened the Harriet Tubman Home for The Aged and Indigent Colored People.

Tubman was the first African-American to join the military. She worked tirelessly with Susan B. Anthony to free slaves over her entire career.

Rosa Parks

Called "The Mother of the Movement," Rosa Parks was a civil rights activist who refused to surrender her seat to a white passenger on a segregated bus in Montgomery, Alabama in 1955.

Her defiance sparked the Montgomery Bus Boycott. Its success launched nationwide efforts to end racial segregation of public facilities.

For her courage, she was awarded the Presidential Medal of Freedom.

John Wayne

"Duke" was my favorite patriot both in films and in real life. His movie credits were saturated with Americana, including "The Quiet Man", "The Horse Soldiers", "The Longest Day", "The Alamo" and Green Berets.

He also hosted an iconic television special entitled, ***"Swing Out, Sweet Land"*** featuring all the top movie and television stars of that day: Lucille Ball, Glen Campbell, the cast of "Bonanza," Jack Benny, Rick, and David Nelson, Ann Margret, Bob Hope, Dean Martin, Tommy Smothers, Dennis Weaver, Bing Crosby, Red Skelton, Johnny Cash, and others.

His comment about the tribute was, "This is my country and I'm going to do good for it!"

Wayne was awarded the Presidential Medal of Honor.

Bob Hope

His USO Christmas shows were a holiday staple every year as he not only honored our troops but also made them laugh!

From Southeast Asia to Saudi Arabia to Greenland to Guantanamo Bay, Bob was everywhere, raising the morale of our soldiers.

You don't get any more patriotic than that!

George M. Cohan

A Congressional Medal of Honor winner, Cohan is the architect of the most legendary patriotic songs in American history!

"Yankee Doodle Boy," "Over There," "You're a Grand Old Flag," and "I'd Rather Be Right!"

Audie Murphy

One of America's most decorated war heroes. Murphy personally took out 241 Nazi soldiers in World War II.

He was awarded 37 medals and decorations, including the Distinguished Service Cross, the Silver Star (with oak leaf cluster), the Legion of Merit, and the Croix de Guerre (with palm).

Sergeant York

In World War I, on October 8, 1918, United States Corporal Alvin C. York killed over 20 German soldiers and captured an additional 132 at the head of a small detachment in the Argonne Forest near the Meuse River in France. The exploits later earned York the Medal of Honor.

Jesse Owens

At the 1936 Olympic Games in Berlin, Owens personally wrecked the pride of Nazi athleticism by winning four gold medals while Hitler sat in the stands and agonized.

Jesse won the 100 meters, the 200 meters, the long jump, and the 4x100 American team relay. He was the first athlete to win four gold medals as he crushed the myth of Nazi superiority.

Jackie Robinson

In 1947, Jackie was the first African American to play Major League baseball. He was told not to retaliate when the white bigots baited him for the first three years, and he kept his promise to Branch Rickey and the Brooklyn Dodgers.

It was an admirable exercise in patriotism because it paved the way for players of color to become part of baseball.

Tuskegee Airmen

The Tuskegee Airmen were the first black military aviators in the U.S. Army Air Corps (AAC), a precursor of the U.S. Air Force. Their impressive performance earned them more than 150 Distinguished Flying Crosses and helped encourage the eventual integration of the U.S. armed forces.

They proved that Black men could fly advanced aircraft in combat as well as their white counterparts.

Norman Schwarzkopf

When Iraq invaded and occupied Kuwait in August 1990, Schwarzkopf directed a buildup of 700,000 U.S., European, and Arab troops in Saudi Arabia to confront the Iraqis.

Under his command, beginning on January 16, 1991, allied forces carried out a six-week-long air bombardment of Iraq and its positions in Kuwait.

In a ground campaign that began on February 24 and lasted only 100 hours, allied forces speedily retook Kuwait and destroyed or incapacitated most of the Iraqi army while sustaining only minimal casualties themselves.

And a special shout out to Ray Charles, whose rendition of "America the Beautiful" is the most stirring version of all time!

No one did it better, God bless you Ray, and thank you.

CHAPTER TWENTY-FIVE

MY PERSONAL HOPES AND ASPIRATIONS FOR MY BELOVED CHILDREN

"When I tell my children that I love them it isn't a habit, it is my constant reminder to them that they are the best thing that has ever happened to me."

My hopes for them…

Being healthy

My first hope for each of you, as my kids, is that you live a full and healthy life. With Covid-19 out there along with all the other diseases, I never want you to suffer in any way.

That's probably unrealistic, so let's just say that I want you to feel vibrant and safe every day of your lives.

I pray you will eat well, sleep eight hours a night, stay away from alcohol and drugs, take vitamins, find a good doctor, and surround yourself with responsible friends who want the best for their lives, as well.

We can't avoid illness, but we can work hard to minimize it. That is my wish for you as your dad.

To seek truth and not happiness

Most parents are always telling their children, "Honey, we just want you to be HAPPY!"

But chasing after happiness is not the end-all. There is a higher value in life than being happy.

It is called *truth.*

Truth is the ethical conscience that guides us. It is the compass of right and wrong. Seeking life's pleasures may make you temporarily happy but that should not be our goal.

Getting drunk at a party or being sexually involved with someone may be the touchstone of happiness but that doesn't make it right.

I want you, as my children, to pursue righteousness, to develop character, integrity and to always take personal responsibility for your actions.

That will not always make you happy at the moment, but it will bring satisfying joy to you in the long run.

I want you to discover your talents in life. If you can figure out your areas of strength, you can be successful in a career that maximizes your value.

As Socrates so succinctly put it,

"Know thyself."

As you launch out into your field of expertise, it is my hope that you will be supported and encouraged to pursue your strengths.

I pray that you, as my sons and daughters, will find strong people to "build a fence of protection" around your lives and help you along life's way.

I want you, as my children, to persevere and fight with a passion to see it through to the end. Anyone can start a race, I want you to be *finishers.*

The champion goes the extra mile and is the last one standing.

Great athletes like Michael Jordan, Kobe Bryant, Muhammad Ali, Billie Jean King, Katie Ledecky, Tom Brady, Lindsey Vonn, among others, were successful not just because of their talent, but because they never quit in the middle of a race or a game.

I want you to be fighters. If it's worth dying for, never take it casually. Press on to the end!

It's important for me to see all of you feeling safe and secure within your family unit. I want your children to develop rich relationships with you as their parents and siblings.

These are the bonds that last.

If you fall short or fail in some way, I always want you to *know* you have a dad who still believes in you and will support you no matter what you do.

When it comes to choosing friends, my hope is that you will find best buddies that are honest, unselfish, have high ethical standards and are always trying to improve themselves in life.

I want you, as my children, to be tolerant and not judge others by the color of their skin or the belief of their religion but to value and respect others in a diversified world.

I hope you will not be afraid to fail. Failure is not a fault, it is when you lie there and let it defeat you that is the problem. Jump back up and do it better the next time!

I hope and pray you will find your life partner who is perfect for you and who loves you unconditionally and will always cherish you in every way.

I would be thrilled if each of you realized your ultimate dreams someday as adults.

And finally, I hope you will always respect your country and revere your God wherever you go.

I want you to be patriotic and proud and love America.

I want you to obey your Sovereign God until your last breath.

And remember this, falling down does not make you a failure, staying down does.

I love you, my children. Always and forever…Dad.

EPILOGUE

In a message to Congress on December 1, 1862, President Abraham Lincoln warned, "We shall nobly save, or meanly lose, the last best hope on heath." President Lincoln's warning has never been more urgent than it is today. I think many people have a false sense of security, thinking that America is invulnerable because of her strong economy, strong military, and strong traditions. As much as I love America, I think she could be swept into the dustbin of history within our lifetime - and I believe it will happen if we allow it.

As a loyal adopted son of this land, and as someone who deeply loves and reverse America's history, I mourn what I am witnessing today. I see my beloved land succumbing to moral decay. I see this "last best hope of earth" at the brink of an abyss. Her citizens, memorized by feelings, are mindlessly pushing her toward that brink. (Michel Youssef Ph.D.)

ABOUT THE AUTHOR

Richard Lira was raised in Los Angeles, California and has attended several colleges and Universities, his range of studies are Political Science, Forensic Physiology and counter-terrorism. He is a father, son, and brother who is strongly invested in our Lord and loves his country very much, he believes in helping those who are less fortunate. He is a veteran who has served his country as a member of the famed 82nd Airborne division as a Brigade sniper, he is also a retired public servant who has served his community with several police agencies before he retired after twenty three years of service. He has provided personnel security for some of the biggest names in the entertainment world like Mariah Carey, Stevie Wonder, Santana, Micheal Jackson to name a few, but most of all, he is an American son.